# Truthful Living

*Saint Benedict's Teaching
on Humility*

Michael Casey

LIBRARY OF CONGRESS CATALOGING-IN-PUBLICATION
DATA

Casey, Michael, monk of Tarrawarra.
    Truthful living : Saint Benedict's teaching on
humility. Michael Casey.
      p. cm.
    Includes bibliographical references.
    ISBN 1-879007-35-5 (pbk.)
    1. Benedict, Saint, Abbot of Monte Cassino. Regula.
2. Humility. Christianity--History of doctrines. 3.
Benedict, Saint, Abbot of Monte Cassino--
Contributions in concept of humility. I. Title.
BX3004.Z5C34 1998
265' . 106--dt21                       98--44323
                                               CIP

Published by:     St. Bede's Publications
                   271 N. Main St.
                   PO Box 545
                   Petersham, MA 01366-0545

# Contents

# Foreword

I offer you these reflections on St Benedict's chapter on humility as a stimulus for your own meditation on this text. I have never found it an easy chapter to come to grips with, despite having worked with it many times since my first attempt in 1974. Nor have I attempted to say the last word in these pages. I simply invite you to join me in interacting with what St Benedict has written, trying to make sense of it and to hear in these sometimes daunting words the call of the Gospel. As always, we hear the challenge according to our own situation and for most of us, this means in the context of a world far different from what Benedict knew.

I have tried to keep abreast of existing scholarship on the Rule of Benedict and on this chapter in particular, and to allow it to influence my thinking. I have not, however, aimed at writing a scholarly commentary, but simply to begin with you, the reader, the process of a critical and practical reflection on an important evangelical principle.

I would like to express my appreciation to all those groups in many countries working with whom I have developed these thoughts. May I say that it has been your interest and encouragement that have motivated me to attempt a more systematic elaboration of the things we spoke about together. Thank you.

# ABBREVIATIONS

ABR ............................ American Benedictine Review
ASOC .............. Analecta Sacri Ordinis Cisterciensis,
later Analecta
Cisterciensia
CFS ................. Cistercian Fathers Series (Kalamazoo)
COCR .............. Collectanea Ordinis Cisterciensium
Reformatorum, later Collectanea
Cisterciensia
CChr ............... Corpus Christianorum, Series Latina
CSQ ................................. Cistercian Studies,
later Cistercian Studies
Quarterly
CSS ................ Cistercian Studies Series (Kalamazoo)
DSp .............................. Dictionnaire de Spiritualité
PL .................................... Patrologia Latina
RB ...................................... Rule of Benedict
RBS ................................... Regulae Benedicti Studia
RM .............................. Rule of the Master
SBOp ..................................... Sancti Bernardi Opera:
The Works of Bernard of
Clairvaux
Adv ............................... Sermons for Advent
Apo .............................. Treatise: Apologia
Dil .............................. Treatise: On the Love of God
Ep ................................................. Letters
Hum .. Treatise: On the Steps of Humility and Pride
Humb ................. Sermon on the Death of Humbert
Quad ............................... Sermons on Lent
SC ............................ Sermons on the Song of Songs
SChr ............................................ Sources Chrétiennes

# I
# Finding a Way to Humility

Humility is a beautiful quality to find in a person. It is a characteristic feature of those who have not forgotten their roots. The term "humility" is related to the word *humus* and points to a connectedness with the earth and, by extension, with all that inhabits the earthly sphere. The book of Genesis reminds us that our race originated from the soil of earth: adam from *admah*; humanity from *humus*. Humble people are down to earth, they are not alienated from their own nature. They accept their origins and are content to be what they are.

A first approach to understanding humility is to see it as that total self-acceptance typical of untarnished humanity. Those who are humble experience no shame. They do not need lies and evasions to inflate their importance in the eyes of their associates, or to buttress their self-esteem. They have overcome the tendency to regard others as competitors or rivals, and so they work with whatever they have, and waste no time envying those who possess different qualities. The humble are equally content with both the gifts and the limitations that come from their nature or their personal history. Humility brings with it a fundamental happiness that is able to cope with external difficulties and sorrows.

The humble are the people about whom Jesus spoke in the Sermon on the Mount: the poor in spirit, the meek, the oppressed. If we regard the Beatitudes as expressive of the philosophy Jesus himself lived, then these sayings can be considered as autobiographical. Jesus is the supreme example of humanity uncomplicated by sin. He is the model of this quality to which we give the name "humility". This is why he said, "Learn of me, for I am meek and humble of heart" (Mt 11:29). Taking together all the New Testament texts that speak of the humility of Jesus, from the kenosis of Philippians 2:7 to the washing of the disciples' feet in John 13, we are led to recognize a distinctive mark of Jesus' personal style. So much so that, perhaps, we can substitute another word for this quality: Christlikeness. Humility is that network of attitudes that springs from a radical conversion of heart, and signals a deep, inner conformity with Christ. Growth in humility is powered by the simple desire to become like Christ.

## 1. Our Difficulty with Humility

For many people humility does not seem like an appropriate ideal. This was true for the ancient Greeks, and it certainly corresponds to the way many of our con-temporaries feel. The word itself engenders strong negative reactions, since it seems to point to a world of values which negates many of the most cherished advances in recent self-understanding. The idea of "humility" evokes the image of a moral tyranny which imparts only fear, guilt and an abiding sense of failure. It has nothing of encouragement or warmth to offer, only a carping insistence on human sinfulness. The robust hyperbole of some traditional writers does not help the situation; frequently their writings provoke only irritation and rejection on the part of modern readers.

This reluctance to accept humility as a desirable quality is apparent even within the Church. There is a certain resentment among those who feel excluded from full participation in communion or ministry whenever they are advised to be quiet or patient and not to rock the boat. Discussion of issues, difference of opinion, dissent, intervention and initiative have not always been encouraged among the people of God. Even though both Inquisition and Index have been officially discontinued, there is still much moral pressure to conform with precedent and current practice. Nor is it unusual to find exhortations to humility and obedience coupled with a disregard for the rights of persons and a practical denial of participative structures within the Church. I think we have to confess that ecclesiastics of all ranks have been known to use the preaching of humility to bludgeon unruly persons into submission. No wonder many who listen to such homilies are suspicious of the motives behind the recommendations.

Besides these "political" difficulties, there are other objections that are more attitudinal. Most Christians of the late twentieth century tend to approach spirituality from a more positive standpoint. We want to be liberated from the lingering after-effects of Jansenism with its emphasis on sin-avoidance, guilt and the fear of punishment. There is a certain interest in self-improvement, but it is fueled by a desire for personal fulfillment rather than by an awareness of personal shortcomings. Freedom, self-expression and responsibility are themes that attract us. The basic goodness of God's creation in all its aspects seems more important than the minor blemishes induced by human weakness. Honesty, authenticity and truth demand that we recognize our failures, but there is no reason to construct our whole life around what has gone wrong.

Before attempting to discuss traditional monastic teaching on humility it is necessary for us as readers to come to grips with our latent resistance. The text of Benedict's Rule is stark and demanding. Our first impulse is to see this chapter as an expression of a spirituality that is no longer acceptable. It is hard to understand why a vibrant spiritual tradition that has exercised such a creative influence in the Church for nearly fifteen centuries should stem from a document that sometimes seems dour, authoritarian and negative. The chapter on humility, by its length and position in the Rule is arguably the heart of Benedict's presentation of the way to God, yet at first approach it seems pessimistic and even vaguely misanthropic.

There is no doubt that St Benedict's triad of humility-silence-obedience is not wildly popular among those with a late twentieth-century Western mentality. Although we admit the unattractiveness of vanity, verbosity and rebellion, we do not place a very high priority on the qualities that are their opposites. This means that we experience a resistance when we come to read Benedict's text. We do not want to waste time with it and prefer to read something more positive. Deliberately seeking lowliness seems like humbug. We want to let our lights shine forth, not to hide them from sight.

Here we must recall an important principle that operates when we read the great works of antiquity. The texts that at first appear unattractive are often the ones that will most repay the effort to understand them. "The argument or example that seems irrelevant, trivial, or boring is precisely the one most likely to be the sign of what is outside of one's framework and which calls it into question."[1] There is an unconscious antagonism in us to anything that threatens our ingrained prejudices, and challenges us to grow. Because we are reluctant to admit our intolerance of a different viewpoint, we project the problem onto the text and proclaim, "This is a hard saying and who can bear with it?" We blame the text for our unwillingness to receive.

A much more creative way of dealing with difficult texts is to take our negative reaction as an indication that there may be an issue beneath the surface with which we must deal. So we return to the text, reading it very closely, word by word, and line by line. "The hardest thing of all is the simplest to formulate: every word must be understood. It is hard because the eye tends to skip over just those things which are most shocking or most call into question our way of looking at things."[2]

The first word of Benedict's Rule is "Listen". We need to learn the art of listening to what St Benedict has to say— not to dismiss his words unheeded because of prejudice or hasty impressions. This means spending time learning his dialect—learning his code—exactly as we have to invest effort in acquiring a taste for an unfamiliar piece of music. This is how Neville Cardus described the process.

> We must always listen patiently to a new work. We need not accept it after we have got to know it. There's no virtue in modernity merely for the sake of being modern. But we must first of all listen to new music—listen to it until we know it as well as the masterpieces we like. We cannot

say we do not like anything—if we do not know it. Unfamiliarity sometimes breeds contempt.[3]

First we need to clarify our own ideas about humility and to identify some of our prejudices. After that we need to give time to finding the authentic meaning of the Rule. Only then do we make a judgment concerning its applicability to the changed circumstances of our own day. By following such a method, we will be able to open the Rule to dialogue with contemporary sensibilities and so achieve some "fusion of horizons". The questions posed by our own age may lead thus to an understanding of latent meanings in the text of the Rule and perhaps to a new appreciation of its author's spiritual wisdom.

## 2. Legitimate Reservations about Humility

Let us examine some further reasons for our lack of enthusiasm. There is no need for us to be defensive about difficulties experienced in understanding Benedict's chapter. The problems that present themselves can be of service in reminding us of the need for clarity and qualification in speaking about such an important topic. After all, there is nothing inherently impossible in thinking that human understanding may have made progress in the 1500 years since Benedict lived.

### a) Passivity

As a program of life, Benedictine humility appears too passive. It seems mainly concerned with the avoidance of sin and offers little encouragement to the doing of good. Attention is turned inward to scrutinize thoughts and instinctual desires. There is a danger of changing a normal human being into someone excessively introspective and even scrupulous. The result of this for many persons is paralysis and inactivity. Furthermore, without the encouragement that follows some perceptible success in doing good, a constant awareness of one's own failures often leads to timidity and depression. Even if we do not go the full distance down this particular road, the whole climate of life produced by such a spirituality is dismal: joyless, without creativity and knowing little of the carefree existence of one who is loved by God.

*b) Evangelization*

A perceived absence of a sense of mission in the Rule of Benedict tends to raise this passivity to the level of infidelity to the call to evangelization. The monk who takes this chapter literally, is so concerned to scrape himself clean from imperfect motivations that he forgets everything outside himself. A spirituality concerned only with inward states and dispositions isolates the individual from the Church's mission, and reduces the kingdom of God to one's private struggles for probity and peace. No doubt this is why the monastic microcosm often mistakes molehills for mountains. Meanwhile there is a systematic inadvertence to many of the essential challenges of the Gospel. The fact that Matthew's picture of the Final Judgment does not inspire a certain uneasiness in monks and nuns must give us pause. How is it that we who profess to pursue an evangelical life exclude from our normal lifestyle the very activities on which Christians will be assessed? Most of us are not personally involved in feeding the hungry, clothing the naked or visiting gaols. By what means do we rationalize such massive omission? Staying at home, keeping silence and following orders are scarcely substitutes for objective conformity with the teaching of Christ. You would think that monastics might have the decency sometimes to feel a little disturbed at the ambiguity of their profession.

*c) Temperament*

Some people are mild and unassertive by temperament. There is no point in preaching "humility" to those who have no need of it. This was recognized by St Gregory the Great in his Pastoral Rule. He concluded that while it is useful to recommend greater reserve to the boisterous and self-confident, it is better to proclaim the opposite virtues to those who are already gentle and perhaps a little timid. In his view spiritual progress operates in a dialectical way. The qualities we need to develop are complementary to those we already have. Everyone is challenged to go beyond the limits dictated by nature and upbringing.

It seems better not to associate humility with particular personality types. Humility is a quality to be pursued by all. So, we have to arrive at a definition of humility that embraces different temperaments and represents a real challenge for everyone. It is also obvious that a more robust ideal is necessary if humility is to be marketed. Few see any value in becoming quiet little mousy people, timorous and unobtrusive to the point of invisibility. Care must be taken to demonstrate that there is also a form of humility that can operate for people who are naturally assertive and articulate. It is surely a mistake automatically to exclude from the ranks of those who embody the qualities of Jesus Christ, prophets, creative trouble-makers and those who are tireless in clamoring for justice.

### d) Premature Old Age

It has been noted that most of the manifestations of humility described by St Benedict and other writers of the monastic tradition are not virtues but simply the result of the slowing-down that comes with old age. The young are typically active and adventurous, boisterously self-assertive and they make a lot of noise. The old prefer their settled bachelor routines, a quiet corner and the abandonment of all initiative and ambition. They are obedient, because they have learned how to bend obedience to their own whims. They have nothing to hide, because most of the vigor of vice has seeped away. Fear of the Lord is not difficult, since the thinning ranks of their contemporaries is a constant intimation of mortality.

Is St Benedict trying to eliminate youthfulness from the community? By pushing the young towards such *gravitas*, is he suppressing the vitality necessary for continuing growth? These are questions worth posing. In the history of most communities there are periods in which the monastery is well-served by the imperfectly-motivated enthusiasm of those who retain the strength and ardor of youth. Yes, sometimes there is self-importance and arrogance, but life itself gradually leaches out such immaturity. On the other hand, there is a danger that in eliminating vice the virtues will have no chance to develop. As St Benedict warns the abbot, "Don't be too zealous in scraping off the rust, lest you put a hole in the vessel" (64.13).[4] It is a sad community where monastic silence is not sometimes disturbed by the energy and laughter of the young. Even worse is the situation where newcomers become accomplices of their own oppression, and allow themselves to be socialized into a system that lacks human authenticity.

### e) Low Self-Esteem

It has been noted that many people today suffer from a poor self-image. Sad to say, many of us pass through phases of self-rejection and even self-hatred. To grow through these periods, we need to be taught self-acceptance and an appropriate level of self-love. We may need to acquire skills of assertiveness to boost our confidence in our own worth and ability. Otherwise we begin to feel so bad about ourselves that anger and sadness become constant companions. In such situations, recommending "humility" is disastrous. Until we become more assured there is no point in advocating a program of ego-denial. The counterpoise is lacking and the result will be imbalance. Any attempt to practice "humility" will only reinforce the sense of worthlessness; it will create a time-bomb of resentment more destructive than any minor acts of self-importance.

Ironically, those who suffer most from a negative self-image will embrace "humility" immediately. It will seem to them to confirm all they have long suspected of themselves: that they are below par, worthless and incompetent—at least in the things that matter. Because, in the last analysis, such people see themselves as unlovable, they sometimes embrace a "spiritual" life or enter religious congregations to compensate for the affirmation that life denies them. Those looking after them will find that first they have to build up the ego, so long crippled by undiagnosed self-rejection. Otherwise outward behavior that seems to indicate humility will be mere sham. Feigned humility does not liberate, it enslaves. It is not the gospel value, it is a devouring lion disguised as a lamb.

### f) Institutionalism

Humility appears to be the handmaid of an institutional approach to living the Christian life: where particular persons are worth nothing apart from their conformity with universal norms and expectations. Instead of a community of brothers and sisters whose differences are a cause for celebration, conformity is enforced. There is a preference for an institutional anonymity, in which everything that is "singular" is systematically eliminated. Mediocrity is the norm. What remains are diminished human beings living according to a lowest common denominator of adherence to corporate standards, even when it is clear that these are not creative for everyone.

When humility, obedience and silence are propounded from on high as the foundation of a way of life, there is always a danger that these "virtues" are

perceived as a means of ensuring a hassle-free existence for superiors. If the criterion of a good monk is
that he does what he is told, remains unassertive and
keeps his mouth shut, then there will certainly be fewer
disturbances of the "peace" of the community: no un-
solicited suggestions, no criticisms, no complaints.
Everything will be under control. Difficulties will be
denied or repressed and revolutions will be unthought
of. Nevertheless, this semblance of a quiet life may
well be an illusion. Such eloquence can be a cloak for
tyranny: not a few monasteries are ruled by a rod of
iron supported by a velvet tongue. More often, perhaps, the ideology of humility is used as a means of
covering up administrative incompetence. Any objections to failures in communication, policy-making or
necessary forethought are put down by an immediate
appeal to patience and submissiveness. The notion of
participative community is easily excluded if the seventh chapter of Benedict's Rule is the only chapter we
read.

Because of the Church's long resistance to egali-
tarian ideals and its tendency to ally itself with the
status quo, cases of injustice and abuse have not been
met with vigorous correction. One of the unstated
rules of the game is that higher authority generally
protects lower authority so that appeals have only
a limited chance of success. As a result, there is
always a suspicion that spiritual ideals such as humility are being proclaimed as a substitute for direct
action to remedy the situation. Religion is being used
as a tranquilizer, so as to leave intact structures of
government that are oppressive to some or even to

a majority. In such a context, praise of humility, obedience and docility is seen by many as being no more than the institution defending itself against change and necessary reform. Sometimes—it has to be said—a grievance is dismissed because prophets are not always "humble" people, especially in the eyes of those whose inaction they condemn. The result, in all these cases, is to give humility a bad name.

### g) Cultures of Compliance

In certain traditional societies and sub-cultures, as in many service industries, much importance is attached to external practices that seem to betoken humility. Servants make their superiors feel good by being totally agreeable: always smiling no matter how they feel. In many countries, compliance, deferment and passivity are expected of those who occupy the lowlier levels of society. In families where parental love is made conditional on children being "good", the same dynamic operates. In such situations "humility" becomes a facade that conceals the real dispositions. Appeasement of superiors becomes a major tactic of survival. When these skills are found in a monastic situation a very hollow person results. External conformity and pleasant manners cause a gnawing inner sense of alienation to go unnoticed. Real difficulties are concealed. Frustration, anger and resentment are driven underground and personal conscience is replaced by a need for approval by superiors. Like other forms of false humility, feigned compliance is hard to discern. It is such an agreeable change to find someone cheerful and obliging that we don't always test to see how genuine the attitude is. When the volcano eventually erupts, it usually catches us by surprise.

### h) Patriarchy

Saint Benedict was a man and he wrote for monks. The humility he advocated was formulated as a means of dealing with personal propensities that are, perhaps, more emphatically masculine. It has been suggested that men have a genetic predisposition to assertiveness and even aggression that has been reinforced by "patriarchal" societies. Men have to learn meekness and gentleness— it does not come naturally. The situation is reversed for women, so the argument goes. Are we to conclude that the Rule of Benedict, since it was written for men, is unsuitable for women? It is not for a man to answer this question. Let readers decide for themselves. All I can say is that Benedict imposes his Rule on no one. He insists that the candidate understand the meaning of the Rule before he obliges himself to it: "Here is the law under which you want to fight: if you can keep it enter. Otherwise freely depart" (58.10). If the cap fits, wear it!

### i) Humility and Humiliation

There is a certain amount of confusion about the relationship between humility and humiliation. In the past, some religious communities embraced a program of systematic humiliation in order to "break" the egotism of new recruits, to socialize them into the community's way of doing things and to punish any deviance from accepted norms. Such penances were widely believed to induce humility. Some of those who submitted to such routine belittling of themselves may have grown in steadfastness. For most, it was probably a matter of enduring because they had no alternative. Those who survive were often scarred by the experience. The result was not humility, but a deep-seated resentment of the treatment they received. Again, real humility has not been well-served by having such institutional power-games associated with it.

## 3. An Approach to Humility

Even though we may not fully agree with the reservations given above or the way in which they are expressed, it can only be helpful to be aware of problems and to take them into account in interpreting St Benedict's Rule. What we are trying to do in this present study is to provide a bridge between an ancient text and the present day. If it is true that receptivity is measured by the capacity of the recipients, then we need to be aware of whatever may restrict this capacity. On the other hand, it may be that our contemporary doubts derive from insights which St Benedict did not have. In which case we can be invited to complete what he wrote in order to arrive at a fuller truth.[5]

There is one area in which we moderns differ substantially from St Benedict and from his medieval successors. Although the Greek New Testament distinguishes humility as humble condition (Lk 2:48) from "humble-mindedness" (e.g. Eph 4:2) the same Latin word is used to translate both. Since the sixteenth century, especially, we have become more attuned to subjective factors. For St Bernard, for example, humility would have seemed to have been a matter of objective lifestyle than of a psychological stance. A monk was humble in so far as he embraced "hard work, a hidden life and voluntary poverty".[6] Today humility seems more like a matter of a particular subjective attitude towards ourselves and others. For us to understand humility we need to use the insights from some of the behavioral sciences. In this book I have tried to effect some fusion of horizons between Benedict and the twentieth century. May my intuitive leaps, anachronisms and occasional flippancies be pardoned!

The way to resolving the dilemma caused by the cultural abyss is by an act of faith: to take seriously St Benedict's claim to be regarded as a spiritual master and to be prepared to listen to his teaching appreciatively. When we have heard what he is saying, then we can decide on its relevance to our own lives. To some extent this will mean penetrating the barrier posed by a language that has become stale in the centuries following St Benedict's death. It will involve going beyond the cultural forms envisaged by Benedict to try to find in our own experience a reflection of the realities to which the Rule refers. We will soon discover that coming to truth may well involve accepting a challenge to many of our settled prejudgements and allowing ourselves to view matters from another standpoint. Reading an ancient text has many similarities to having discussion with a person from another culture; the insight gained is often in direct proportion to the effort we make to understand a question from another angle. We can be enriched by reading a sixth century document because it throws light on the blind spots we have from our own cultural attitudes.

I am proposing a very active reading of Benedict's Rule. I do not recommend the automatic acceptance of everything he has to say, but I ask the reader to accompany me as I struggle to make sense of a text that sometimes seems ill-advised. I invite you to draw on your own experience in trying to establish a context for Benedict's remarks, pausing as you read to reflect on your own life and what you have learned in the course of it.

One thing I have found necessary for myself is to keep in mind the fundamental dialectic of life and death in the Christian experience. There can be no genuine spirituality that does not take seriously the gospel imperative of the paschal mystery. We enter life through the doorway of death. Receptivity of grace involves the diminishment of certain temporal advantages. It could be said that it involves a loss of self. It is impossible to understand the reality of humility or the teaching of St Benedict if we do not accept this basic principle.[7]

My method in this book will be to take the text of St Benedict's chapter on humility, to try to understand its literal meaning on the basis of available scholarship and then to consider different themes that the text suggests. In this reflection I will be drawing on my own experience of monastic realities as well as that of others. My aim is to arrive at a point where I will have something that addresses practical reality. My desired goal is to bring into the light "moral goodness and basic monasticity" (RB 73.1). In other words, the interpretation I am offering is primarily monastic as distinct from scholarly.[8]

After some hesitation I have decided to leave St Benedict's words in the context of a conventional monastery of monks. At the same time, I would hope that these reflections will make sense to a much wider readership. I encourage layfolk, women and those who belong to a non-Western culture to attempt to enter into the original context of the Rule with me, and I hope that they will find there something worthwhile to carry back to their own situation.

Because of my practical goal this is a very concrete book. Many of the examples I use come from my experience. I have changed the details and usually indulged in some exaggeration to make the point clearer. Bernard of Clairvaux defended his use of unflattering examples in his work on *The Steps of Humility and Pride* by saying that he was personally more acquainted with the way down than with the way up.[9] Like Bernard, I hope that the occasional caricatures that I draw cause a smile of recognition rather than a surge of resentment. The fact is that we often learn about an unknown good by looking at a known evil.

### Notes

[1] Allan Bloom, "The Study of Texts" in *Giants and Dwarfs: Essays 1960-1990* (New York: Simon and Schuster, 1990), pp. 308.

[2] Ibid.

[3] Quoted by Geoffrey Tozer in *ABC Radio 24 Hours*, January 1998, p. 15.

[4] Citations of Benedict's Rule (RB) are given by chapter and verse. The system of division followed here is that used by most modern translations.

[5] Perhaps our unease with a text results from a pre-conceptual sense of right and wrong that needs to be respected. As Leon Kass argued in "The Wisdom of Repugnance," sometimes "repugnance is the emotional expression of deep wisdom, beyond reason's power fully to articulate." Quoted in *Quadrant* 41.12 (December 1997), p. 50.

[6] Ep 42.37; SBOp 7.130.21: *Labor et latebrae et voluntaria paupertas, haec sunt monachorum insignia.*

[7] See Thomas X. Davis, "Loss of Self in the Degrees of Humility in the Rule of Saint Benedict, Chapter VII," in E. Rozanne Elder [ed.], *Benedictus: Studies in Honor of St Benedict of Nursia* (CSS 67; Cistercian Publications, Kalamazoo, 1981), pp. 23-29.

[8] Those who are interested in the theoretical basis of monastic hermeneutics, as I understand it, may consult some of my articles on this topic. "Variations on a Theme: Approach to the Rule," *Tjurunga* 2 (1971), pp. 5-11. "The Hard Sayings of the Rule of Benedict," *Tjurunga* 3 (1972), pp. 133-143. "The Hermeneutics of Tradition," *Tjurunga* 5 (1973), pp. 39-50. "Principles of Interpretation and Application of the Rule of Benedict," *Tjurunga* 14 (1977), pp. 33-38; reprinted as "RB: Then and Now," in *Benedictines* 36.2 (1981), pp. 10-15."Orthopraxy and Interpretation," *RBS* 14/15 (1985/86), pp. 165-172. Much of this issue of *RBS* is dedicated to the question of Hermeneutics. For a survey that indicates how my approach compares with other contemporary strategies, see Kurt Belsole, "The Regula Benedicti: Perspectives on Interpretation,"*ABR* 48.1 (1997), pp. 19-51

[9] Hum 57; SBOp 3.38.18-19. There is an English translation of this entertaining but wise commentary in Bernard of Clairvaux, *Treatises II* (CFS 13; Cistercian Publications, Washington/Kalamazoo, 1974).

# II
# Humility As Truth

Bernard of Clairvaux clearly affirms that humility is grounded on truth: within oneself, in one's relations with others and with regard to God.[1] This is, perhaps a more positive way of approaching humility, and one which enables us to appreciate its importance. In such a perspective "humility" connotes a fundamental concordance with the reality of one's nature. Pride is more than *hauteur*; it is radical falsehood. In saying this we have to remember that in ancient terms "truth" was viewed as more than correct information. It was seen as a quality of being, taken as a whole, and not merely a state of intellect. It signified the conformity of the created reality with the intention of its Maker. In this context, truth touched not only the mind but also the heart and the emotions. To be alienated from the truth was to be cut adrift from all that makes us human. Separation from truth was seen as the source of all human suffering, the result of the will failing to find its proper object in reality. On a practical level, the ancients understood that a defective grasp of truth inevitably led to positive falsehood. If we are not concerned to pursue and embrace the truth then surely we will be ensnared by its opposite. As Bernard wrote, "The pursuit of empty things amounts to a contempt for the truth, and it is this contempt for the truth that causes our blindness."[2] We will go astray.

Truth-filled living is the soul of humility. It is characterized by an attitude of realism. Humility is, above all, a respect for the nature of things, a reluctance to force reality to conform to subjective factors in ourselves. Applied to human reality, truth's various zones of application can be summarized under the following four headings. These can also be regarded as the foundation of an attitude to life that is characterized by humility.

*a) We are not divine*

In the Garden of Eden the first temptation succeeded because it promised that we should become gods. This desire is the essence of pride. We want to deny our earthly origins with their consequences of vulnerability, weakness, labor, social constraint and limitation. We refuse to be satisfied with a medium level of gratification. We demand a high level of pleasure, total freedom, power, a good reputation and a complete absence of irritants. And we want them now. Whatever gnaws away at our capacity to be happy in the restricted possibilities normal human life offers, may be labeled as the opposite of humility, that is "pride". We demand from others what they cannot possibly give us. We are resentful that they do not give us all that we want. Humility, on the other hand, leads us to find contentment in the ordinary, obscure and laborious occupations that constitute our daily existence.

In forgetting that we are not gods, pride also makes us expect too much from ourselves. Many people cannot forgive themselves for being human: for their slowness of mind and ineffectiveness of will. Their chagrin with their own contingent goodness and their zeal for self-improvement do not constitute humility. They stem from wounded pride. The truth is that we are not divine and so we cannot be expected to perform as gods. The first thrust of humility is to inculcate in us an acceptance that we are of the earth; we are humus. To judge ourselves or others from any other perspective is false, and will eventually become destructive.

*b) We are creatures*

The recognition of our earthly nature leads us to affirm that our fundamental relationship with God is one of dependence. We are not the source of our own being: our race exists only because we receive life from another. However great the divine condescension, we are never on a par with God. Truth in prayer, worship and service of God is characterized by the realization that all that we have comes from God; we have nothing to contribute to the relationship except our needs. Our deepest spiritual experience is to feel utterly dependent on God and to want to submit ourselves to the divine will. The mystics talk about a point at which the soul becomes absorbed in God and seems no longer to have an autonomous existence. God creates. God sustains us in being. Like children who buy Christmas gifts for their parents with money received from them, we can give nothing to God that has not first been God's gift. Far from expecting God to congratulate us for our attempts to lead a good life, we need to recognize the truth of Jesus' saying: "When you have done all that you were ordered, say 'We are unprofitable servants: we have done only what we ought to have done'"(Lk 17:10).

The truth is that our being is incomplete without God. To seek God is, therefore, a fundamental tendency of our nature. "You have made us for yourself and our hearts are restless until they rest in you." We cannot attain human fulfillment except in relationship with God. There is a space in us that can be filled by only God. There is a certain spiritual potentiality that never comes alive if we are locked in a world of self-sufficiency. "Look to God that you may become radiant" (Ps 34:5).

### c) We are sinners

In addition to recognizing the incompleteness of our nature, we need to take account of our personal history of meanness. We have rejected God's advances in many ways and often related to our brothers and sisters with coldness and hostility. None of us is blameless. None of us is in a morally neutral state. We have all incurred liabilities through our sustained selfishness and by our refusal to accept the challenges of growth. We bear within our very being the traces of past infidelity and self-centerdness. As a result we approach God as people who have deformed creation by our futile efforts to replace the reign of God with some silly semblance of self- determination. Sinfulness is not the whole truth about the human condition, but it is certainly a reality. Nobody wants to admit being a sinner, so most of us have to make a conscious effort to discover the reality of sin that is hidden beneath the surface of our well-meaning lives. Otherwise we quickly slide into delusion.

Here it is important to realize that we are speaking of sin more as a theological reality and less as the experience of personal guilt. We are not identifying humanity or human weakness with sin. Instinctual thoughts and desires, no matter how disreputable are not sin. Sin is the free preference for evil over goodness. It is the absurd choice we humans often make for what is intrinsically of less value. Sin is the rejection of the human tendency to seek the good, the beautiful and the true. Sin is, fundamentally, the denial of our nature.

Sin concerns especially the breaking of relationships. When we sin against God, it is not merely a violation of the divine law, but it is a turning away from the God who seeks us, and calls us to fuller life. Like the Prodigal Son we turn away from the warmth of paternal love and lose ourselves in searching for oblivion. It is not a cosmic disaster on a grand scale, but simply a puzzle of personal tragedy. No wonder God regards our aberration, as Julian of Norwich says, "more with pity than with blame".

### d) We are stalled human beings

None of us has had a uninterrupted journey through life. We have all had bad experiences which have led us astray, slowed us down, brought us to a halt or maybe even sent us tumbling backwards. There have been difficulties, mistakes, inconsistencies. Sometimes these are caused by others. Sometimes they are aided and abetted by ourselves. As a result, we adults carry through life a measure of woundedness, although we are rarely conscious of its full magnitude. The fact is that we have not progressed to the extent of our innate potentialities. Many past events continue to have a permanent effect on our lives. We also bear the burden of shame at our own incompleteness. Each one of us has fallen short of the glory of God (Rom 3:23).

Humility involves the acceptance of the liabilities of our personal history as reality. We do not have to approve what others have done to us or the ugliness that we have embraced and the laziness that has left us stagnant. It is a question of recognizing the truth of our present situation as deriving from the past and beginning anew. Pride denies that the past has passed. It ignores present possibilities by constantly reliving former experiences in an effort to correct what is beyond our power to change. It is the kind of perfectionism that cannot accept the approximativeness of most human life. It reminds me of the character in Albert Camus' *The Plague* who keeps rewriting the first sentence of an opus we know will never reach even a few pages. Trying to tinker with the past is an exercise in bad faith. We use former unfairness, for example, as an excuse to refuse the demands of the present. Those who consider themselves victims are often notoriously insensitive to the hurt they inflict on others. In their view, they have been so greatly wronged in the past that the balance of right must be forever on their side, no matter what they do.

If we do not accept the unreality of some of our ideals, it may be that disappointment will make us unwilling to attempt anything bold. Challenges are unwelcome because each choice we make narrows the possibilities for the future. We fear that committing ourselves to one course of action will exclude other desirable possibilities, and we are not ready to make that sacrifice. We will never interact creatively with the present unless we accept that whatever we do will involve leaving aside alternatives and being satisfied with something that may well be imperfect. To marry one is to exclude the rest. On the other hand any imperfect reality is better than the "perfection" that belongs only to the world of fantasy. To exclude the real because it is imperfect is to live a life ensconced in daydreams As the old saying goes, "the best is the enemy of the good". Or in Chesterton's rephrasing of a nineteenth century cliché: "If it is worth doing, it is worth doing badly."

Humility is not all negativity. Quite the contrary, the poignancy of spiritual endeavor is due to the presence in us of lofty desires that are far beyond our range of capability. We have a natural affinity with the spiritual world that even sin cannot unseat. The trouble is that we have no possibility of fulfilling our spiritual aspirations by our own efforts. The more we become conscious of an interior movement towards God, the more defeated we feel if we think that its realization will quickly follow. The process of divinization (as the ancient Church Fathers termed it) is beyond our control. The only means we have of furthering it is to cede control. This will happen only when we affirm with equal conviction that our spiritual giftedness is constantly under threat from an alternative government "that dwells in my members" (Rom 7:23). We cannot pass immediately to God because we are fragmented. At all stages we need's God's help. Humility is what inclines us to accept it.

It is not true that the human condition is one of unmitigated corruption. On the other hand neither is it so that goodness reigns unchallenged. The truth of human life is that we are called to the highest realities and yet often have inclinations that lead us to the lowest. We desire to become divine yet sometimes we allow ourselves to become dehumanized to the point where it is unfair to animals to term our behavior "bestial". The best protection against such a decline is to be aware of its possibility. It is precisely our response to the spiritual energies of our nature that makes us wary of giving in to contrary tendencies.

Humility is truth, and truthful living is most aided by a realistic attitude to ourselves and to others. This means recognizing our common spiritual destiny as also the universal inhibitors that tend to keep all of us grounded. One of the original elements in St Bernard's treatment of humility as truth was the awareness that one of the concomitants of humility is a sense of solidarity with other human beings, compassion, communion. Humility joins us with the rest of the human race. It is pride which causes us to believe that we are not like others, as the Pharisee said in Luke 18:11, that we are exceptions, that the ordinary rules do not apply to us.[3] Pride is the opposite of approachability; it denies every bond that links us with others. Not surprisingly, its power to disrupt community is considerable.

Humility teaches us to recognize that our natural and acquired assets are gifts: they are not of our own making. Furthermore, the gifts we receive are held in trust for the whole human race. They are not for ourselves alone. They are given for sharing. To deny our gifts is to deny others the profit of sharing in their fruits. Such a refusal can have no part in genuine humility.

To accept the truth of our own giftedness in humility obliges us to recognize the measure of responsibility that is part of every personal endowment. If we are artists, we need to work hard to develop our art and also to accept the isolation that often accompanies creativity. If we are companionable people, then we must accept willingly the role of encouragement and peacemaking. If we are cooks, we must roll up our sleeves and head for the kitchen. "As each has received a gift, then use it for one another, as good stewards of God's varied grace" (1 Pet 4:10). Humility does not mean denying gifts; it means making use of them in a spirit of thankfulness and celebration and avowing that what we have is something that has been freely given to us.

Furthermore humility calls us to recognize that God's gifts come sometimes in disguise. This means having faith in a Providence that is active at all times. It leads us to affirm that "God arranges all things whether they appear favorable or not with a view to our welfare".[4] Sometimes we have to subordinate the instinctive evaluation of a situation to our faith that all that happens comes from God's hand and is meant for our good. The lower truth of our immediate reactions must yield to the higher truth of a loving and caring God. Sometimes it is only many years later that the real meaning of events is revealed.

Faith in God's providence is not merely passive resignation in the teeth of disappointment. Humility obliges us to capitalize on the moment that opportunity offers. *Carpe diem!* Too often humility is associated with a fearful refusal to take any initiative or breach any precedent. This is to confuse the evangelical quality with mere timidity. Humility is not restricted to those who have the temperament of a mouse. Nor may it offer any excuse to those whose moral courage is defective. Humility is truth; when opportunity and aptitude coincide, it is humility that impels us to take the risk and act. Humility is not incompatible with the gift of boldness so often mentioned in the Acts of the Apostles. There is, of course, no guarantee of the success of the action or the plaudits of onlookers. Humility helps us to cope with that uncertainty also: the value of a truthful action is not lessened by contingent effects, although it takes a little maturity to recognize this.

If we take the truthfulness of humility seriously, we will come to the conclusion that humility is the opposite of any kind of artificiality, role-playing, good manners or seemliness. The Pharisee, we remember, was condemned for being an *hupocrites*, a word that means a play-actor, pretender, dissembler. Humility means setting aside the mask. It is a kind of nakedness that allows us to be seen without the bulwarks of social conventions. We present ourselves to others transparently, in all our imperfection and vulnerability. We depend on their good will for acceptance and love, not on the success of our efforts at self-promotion.

The fruit of humility, as we shall see when we comment on the end of Benedict's chapter, is naturalness. Being at home with ourselves. Being ourselves. Grace extroverts itself. It begins subtly in the depths of our spirits, but in the course of a lifetime evangelizes all levels of our being until it becomes outward, visible, communicable. It can never reach this point if we are in the habit of hiding behind a facade so that our true self is always concealed.

Bernard of Clairvaux sees the practice of virtue as passing through three stages. It begins at the level of *disciplina*. We have to learn from others what to do in order to be good. After many years virtue becomes habitual, it is second nature to us. This is the level of *natura*. Finally the actions that once cost us so much become not only dutiful or habitual but even gratifying. This is the highest level, the level of *gratia* in which the human being is so transformed that godly acts are no longer a strain but a source of delight.[5]

Here we confront a certain contemporary attitude that equates sin with having a good time. Many people regard religion as something foreign or even hostile to human nature. As a result religion becomes a matter of social conformity, duty and guilt: it is life-denying. There seems little in it that leads to the joyous fulfillment of natural aspirations. Any sort of religious activity can easily be seen as in some way external to the spontaneous yearnings of the human heart. Perhaps as a result of this, there has been a loss in the theological sense of sin. Since religion involved self-denial, wrongdoing became identified with pleasure. The avoidance of gratification began to seem pointless once the external forms that constitute "religion" were dropped. Becoming rich and powerful with no limits placed on the gratification of appetites appears to many as an ideal worth pursuing. Pleasure has become the norm of goodness: "If it feels good, do it." As a result any restraint on pleasure on the basis of non-immediate principles seems like foolishness. The false guilt of the past has led many to deny guilt altogether—even when eminent cause for it exists. The result is a life built on radical untruth.

The fact that most monks and nuns are not mindless seekers of pleasure does not alter the fact that they have been influenced by the philosophy on which contemporary hedonism is based. The effect of half-absorbing such an attitude in the process of growing up is that a monk may be half-hearted in rooting out sin, simply because he half-believes that without "sin" life can only be joyless. A strong level of inconsistency exists between the values he has internalized from society and the style of life he desires and strives to lead.

Accordingly, the opposite case deserves to be stated.
People who sin because of their compulsions, are not having
much fun nor is their life spectacularly fulfilling. They may
experience relief or temporary gratification of one sort or
another, but fundamentally they are unfree. In a sense they
are non-persons. They are being driven by their passions,
both conscious and unconscious. Whatever they may think,
their actions do not derive from the personal center, from
the heart. Their behavior is dictated by their instincts and
by the inner tyranny that results from the mindless
absorption of beliefs and values from outside. A puppet
government controls their conduct. It is not responsible to
them; its allegiance is elsewhere. This is why many people
go through years of agony on the road to conversion. They
feel oppressed by the past they have internalized, yet
simultaneously there is no energy for revolution. Augustine
stated as much.

> Proud persons commit many sins, but not all of
> them are committed proudly. They are defective. Some
> are committed by the ignorant, some by the weak, and
> many of them are done by persons who are weeping and
> grieving. [6]

One of the early experiences on the way to conversion
is the sense of being trapped in sinfulness. Half-desiring an
escape but not perceiving any possible means of release.

> For the eye of the mind is unable to fix itself
> firmly on what it had so fleetingly glimpsed. It is subject
> to the constraint of inveterate habit holding it down.
> In this state the person is filled with yearning and

ardently tries to transcend self. Each time weariness intervenes and the soul sinks back into familiar darkness.[7]

Conversion means being liberated by God's grace so that we can at last follow the intimate spiritual aspirations that have long been unheeded, neglected or frustrated. It is the beginning of the journey towards a fulfillment, a journey powered by the spiritual quest but one which profoundly influences and transforms every sphere of human activity and experience. It is not an irreversible step, nor is it unconditionally guaranteed against breakdown. But it is a beginning. If we work hard at maintaining the process, as far as it depends on us, we can be reasonably sure that it will bring us to a happy conclusion. This is not to say, however, that we will always understand the ways in which we are led.

At the heart of Christian anthropology is the conviction of a deep affinity between human nature and spiritual life. The difficulties of living spiritually do not come from our nature, as such, but from the deformation of our nature through selfishness and pride. Humility aims to eliminate the phony aspects of our life and to help us to live in truth. Part of the truth of human existence is that we are called to live for God. Humility, oddly enough, leads us to recognize our human dignity. It reminds us that we were created for God and that we will be profoundly miserable until we devote the substance of our energies to the realization of this innate potential.

In this chapter, under the influence of St Bernard and others, we have digressed a little from our purpose of explaining the text of the Rule of Benedict. Our reflections have been framed with a view to stimulating our reflection on the global aspects of humility. The time has come now to open the Rule and listen to what St Benedict has to say.

## Notes

[1] Hum 6; SBOp 3.20.14-15.

[2] Ep 18.1: SBOp 7.67.3-4: *Appetitus vanitatis est contemptus veritatis, contemptus veritatis causa nostrae caecitatis.*

[3] "We are all exceptions" cries a character in Albert Camus' *The Fall* (Harmondsworth: Penguin, 1963), p. 60. Freud notes how the claim to being different can be used a means of avoiding the hard tasks necessary for healing and health. "Thus, when one exacts from the patient a readiness to accept some temporary suffering in view of a better end, or even only the resolve to submit to a necessity which applies to all human beings, one will come upon individuals who resist such an appeal on special grounds. They say that they have renounced enough and suffered enough, and have a claim to be spared any further exactions; they will submit no longer to disagreeable necessity for they are exceptions and intend to remain so." *On Creativity and the Unconscious: Papers on the Psychology of Art, Literature, Love, Religion* (San Francisco: Harper and Row, 1958), "Some Character-Types met with in Psycho-Analytic Work," p. 86. Freud traces the claim to the grievance resulting from childhood trauma.

[4] John Cassian, *Conference* 9.20; SChr 54, pp. 57-58.

[5] SC 23.6; SBOp 1.141-142.

[6] Augustine, *De natura et gratia* 29.33; PL 44, 263b.

[7] Gregory the Great, *Moralia* 23.43; PL 76, 277c.

# III
# The Rule of Saint Benedict

Saint Benedict's teaching on humility can be found at various points in his text. His principal exposition of it is in the seventh chapter, comprising 70 verses (or about 8% of the whole Rule). Some foundations were laid in the preceding chapters on obedience and silence and a few qualifications and additions to this basic presentation will be made as Benedict continues with the remaining 66 chapters of his "little rule for beginners". The crux of Benedict's view of humility can be found in his Chapter 7.

To appreciate the exact flavor of Benedict's teaching it is always necessary to view it in the context of his own sources. Benedict was not a very original writer. He was more concerned with compiling a practical handbook for monastic living than in giving perfect expression to his own thought. In addition, he was less concerned with his own creativity than in being faithful to the monastic tradition that had nurtured his own vocation. And so his Rule is a scissors-and-paste job. It is generally agreed that his basic text was an earlier Italian rule known as the Rule of the Master (RM).[1] Benedict's subsequent redaction of his work was often influenced by other texts that he had read, such as the Rule of Augustine and the writings of the great "Catholic Fathers" to whom he refers on more than one occasion.

Because of this complicated method of composition we need to take special precautions to read the Rule within the context of the tradition it embodies. This is not merely a matter of pedigree-hunting designed to amuse the learned. It is necessary, in some degree, for anyone who wants to understand who St Benedict was and what he wrote.[2] More relevantly, perhaps, a more educated approach to the text of the Rule is crucial if we are to avoid misinterpreting what we read. This is not to say that we have to become scholars before we can profit from what St Benedict wrote. It means simply that we need to have the skill of learning from the experts so that we approach the text more sensibly. It is a little like reading the Bible. We need others to translate and annotate the text for us so that we can more easily concentrate on the more important task of applying the Scriptures to our own situation.

Whenever we read the Rule we have to distinguish five kinds of matter:

a) What Benedict took over unchanged from his immediate source, i.e. from RM,

b) Borrowings from RM that Benedict changed in some way,

c) Deliberate omissions from the text of RM,

d) Matter included from other sources, such as Augustine, Basil, Cassian, Cyprian,

e) Benedict's own original contributions.

Once identified, these various literary processes allow us to distinguish different levels of Benedict's involvement in the final version. In some cases he is merely reproducing an existing text against which he has no serious objections. In others he is actively reshaping the material to make it say more exactly what he means. The mind of Benedict can thus be understood more by appreciating his work as editor than by mere analysis of the finished product without reference to the process by which it was formed.

This means that understanding Benedict's position on humility involves reading RB 7 against the background of its main sources: the tenth chapter of the *Rule of the Master* (RM 10) and a section in the *Institutes* of St John Cassian (Book IV, #39).

## 1. Foundation: The Text of John Cassian

John Cassian (360-435) was one of the important channels by which the teaching of the Desert Fathers was reshaped to suit the needs of western monasteries. About 420 he composed a book of *Institutes* for the monastic communities he had founded at Marseille. In the first four books of this work, he discusses the external forms of monastic life and the reception of new recruits. At the end of this material he has inserted a discourse attributed to Abba Pinufius to mark the entry of a novice into the monastic state. Beginning with the theme of renunciation, he moves on to a discussion of fear of the Lord, the beginning of the spiritual process. He then offers ten signs of humility by which the monk's advance from fear to love is verified.[3] Cassian does not speak of a "ladder" of humility, although it is clear that he sees the various moments of spiritual advance in a dynamic sequence.[4] Elsewhere he speaks of series of steps,[5] of first foundations,[6] and goals.[7]

It is in this order and by these stages [or steps] that one arrives at this state of perfection. Here is Cassian's text.[8]

The beginning and end of our salvation as well as its safeguard is fear of the Lord. It is through this that those who give themselves to the way of perfection acquire the beginning of conversion, the cleansing of vices and the safeguarding of the virtues. When fear of the Lord penetrates someone's mind it brings to birth a contempt for all things, forgetfulness of family and a drawing back from the world. The fact is that humility is acquired through contempt for and privation of everything.

[The presence of] humility can be verified by the following indicators:

♦ If [the monk] mortifies in himself all [the movements] of self-will.

♦ If he reveals to his senior not only his actions but also his thoughts

♦ If he allows nothing to his own power of discernment but entrusts everything to the judgment [of the senior] thirsting for his advice and gladly listening to it.

♦ If in all situations he maintains the meekness that is obedience and the constancy that is patience.

♦ If he not only does no injury to anyone but is not grieved and saddened when another inflicts on him an undeserved injury.

♦ If he does nothing and presumes nothing except what is encouraged by the common rule and the example of the superiors.

♦ If he is content with whatever is of little value and in all that is given him to do he regards himself as a wicked and unworthy workman.

♦ If he not only openly declares himself to be inferior to all, but believes it in the very depths of his heart.

♦ If he controls his tongue and does not speak loudly.

♦ If he is not inclined to ready laughter.

By such and other similar indicators true humility can be diagnosed. When it is possessed in truth humility will speedily lead you to the higher level which is the charity that has no fear. Through such charity you will begin to observe effortlessly as if by nature everything that you used to perform with some hardship and trepidation. [You will be motivated] no longer by contemplating punishment or by any fear but by the love of goodness itself and by delight in virtue.

## 2. The Rule of the Master and Benedict

The Rule of the Master (RM 10) converted the ten signs of humility into a ladder of twelve steps. The Master expanded John Cassian's presentation, enriching it with quotations from the New Testament, the Wisdom books and especially the Psalms. The relative density of scriptural citations is an important factor. It signifies that this quality of humility is not merely a social or cultural attitude or way of behaving. It is, rather, the disposition required of all who take the teaching of Christ seriously. "Learn of me for I am meek

and humble of heart" (Mt 11:29), even though—
curiously enough—this particular text is not cited.
Benedict accepts the Master's presentation with few
changes. There are two large omissions to RM which
will be discussed in the commentary. In addition, some
fine tuning is apparent in the addition of three adverbial
phrases that clarify the appropriate dispositions monks
should have in the practice of humility.

Here is the text, as St Benedict completed it. The
translation is my own—with much reliance on previous
translations and commentaries. To slow down the reading
and to begin the process of reflection, I have broken up the
text into smaller sections and attached an introductory word.
I have also indicated the biblical texts that are cited directly.[9]
I have not made the translation inclusive, but have frequently
expanded St Benedict's pronouns by using the word "monk".
This is intended to serve as an occasional reminder of the
original context of this teaching.

## CHAPTER 7: HUMILITY

*St Benedict begins by stating the Scriptural basis for humility: it is the
pre-condition for final "exaltation" by God. Scripture: Lk 14:11,
18.14, Ps 130:1-2.*

1] Brothers, sacred Scripture cries out to us: "All
who exalt themselves will be humbled, and those
who humble themselves will be exalted." 2] This
saying, therefore, demonstrates that all exaltation
is a type of pride. 3] The Prophet shows that he
takes precautions against this by saying: "Lord, my
heart is not exalted and my eyes are not uplifted. I
have not walked in great affairs, nor in marvels that

are beyond me." 4] For what reason? "If instead of feeling humble, I exalted my soul then, like a weaned child on its mother's lap, you would rebuff my soul."

*Humility is a ladder by which we move from earth to heaven.* **Scripture: Gen 28:12.**

5] So, brothers, if we wish to attain the summit of the highest humility, and if we desire to arrive quickly at that heavenly exaltation to which we ascend by the humility of this present life, 6] then a ladder is set up by our ascending actions that Jacob saw in a dream on which there were angels descending and ascending. 7] Without doubt, this descent and ascent is to be understood by us as meaning that we descend by exaltation and ascend by humility. 8] Now the ladder erected is our life on earth that the Lord will raise to heaven for the humbled heart. 9] We may say that our body and soul are the sides of this ladder, into which God's call has placed the various steps of humility and discipline by which we ascend.

*The first step is "fear of the Lord": making a serious effort to live a good life. Scripture: Ps 35:2.*

10] And so the first step of humility is that a monk always keeps the fear of God before his eyes and flees from all forgetfulness. 11] He must always remember all God's instructions. The monk is always to turn over in his mind how all who despise God will fall into hell for their sins, as well as the everlasting life prepared for those who fear God.

12] Let him guard himself at every hour from sins and vices, be they of thought or tongue, of hand or foot, of self-will or fleshly desire. 13] Let the monk consider that at every hour human beings are always seen by God in heaven, that their actions in every place are in God's sight and are reported by angels at every hour.

*We must always be careful about thoughts.* **Scripture: Ps 7:10, 93:11, 138:3, 75:11, 17:24.**

14] The Prophet demonstrates this to us when he shows that God is always present in our thoughts: "God searches hearts and kidneys." 15] Again he says: "The Lord knows the thoughts of human beings." 16] And in the same vein: "You understand my thoughts from afar." 17] And: "Human thoughts will be open before you." 18] That he may be careful about his perverse thoughts, the good brother should always say in his heart: "I shall be blameless before God if I guard myself from my wickedness".

*We must avoid self-will.* **Scripture: Sir 18:30, Mt 6:10, Prov 16:25, Ps 13:1.**

19] Indeed, we are forbidden to do our own will, when Scripture says: "Turn away from your willfulness." 20] Again, in the [Lord's] Prayer we ask God that his will be done in us. 21] We are rightly taught not to do our own will, since we should beware of what Scripture says: "There are ways which seem humanly right whose end plunges into the depths of hell." 22] In addition, we are afraid of what is said about the negligent: "They have been corrupted and have become disgusting in what they choose."

*Pursue not your lusts. Scripture: Ps 37:10, Sir 18:30.*
23] Let us believe that God is always present to us even in the desires of the flesh for, as the Prophet says to the Lord, "All my desire is before you." 24] We must, then, beware of evil desire, because death stands near the entrance of delight. 25] For this reason Scripture instructs us: "Do not pursue your lusts."

*God waits for us to be converted. Scripture: Prov 15:3, Ps 13:2-3, 49:21.*
26] Therefore, because the eyes of the Lord are watching the good and the wicked, 27] and because the Lord is always looking down from heaven on human beings to see whether any understand and seek God; 28] and because every day, day and night, the angels assigned to us report our doings to the Lord 29] then, brothers, we must beware every hour or, as the Prophet says in the Psalm, "God may, at one time, see us falling into evil and become useless. 30] God spares us at this time because he is kind and waits for us to be converted to something better. In the future he may say to us: "You did this, and I was silent."

*The second step is the renunciation of self will and desire. Scripture: Jn 6:38.*
31] The second step of humility is that a monk does not love his own will or delight in the satis-

faction of his desires. 32] Rather he imitates by his
deeds the Lord's saying: "I have come not to do
my own will, but the will of him who sent me."
33] Scripture also says: "Will deserves punishment;
necessity wins a crown."

*The third step is submission to a superior in imitation of Christ.*
*Scripture: Phil 2:8.*
34] The third step of humility is that a monk for
the love of God submits to his superior in all
obedience, imitating the Lord of whom the Apostle
says: "He became obedient until death."

*The fourth step is patience in enduring difficulties with equanimity.*
*Scripture: Mt 10:22, Ps 26:14, Rom 8:36-37, Ps 43:22, Ps*
*65:10-12, Mt 5:39, 2 Cor 11:26, 1 Cor 4:12.*
35] The fourth step of humility is that when this
obedience [involves] hard and contrary things, or
even when there may be undeserved injuries, his
mind quietly embraces patience. 36] He endures
[hardship] without growing weary or running
away. Scripture says: "Those who persevere to the
end will be saved." Again: "Let your heart be
strength-ened; trust in the Lord." 38] Scripture
demonstrates that the faithful, for the Lord's sake,
must bear everything, even contrary things. It says
in the person of the victims: "For your sake we are
afflicted with death all the day long. We are
reckoned as sheep for the slaughter." 39] But secure
in the hope of God's reward, they continue
joyfully: "But in all these things we have overcome
because of him who loved us." 40] Elsewhere

Scripture says: "God, you have tested us, you have tried us as silver is assayed by fire. You led us into a trap and heaped troubles on our backs." 41] Then, to show that we ought to be under a superior, it adds: "You have put human beings over our heads." 42] These are they who fulfill the Lord's command by patience in adversity and injury. When struck on one cheek, they offer the other; they release their cloak to someone who steals their tunic; when forced to go one mile, they go two. 43] With the Apostle Paul, they bear false brothers and persecution, and they bless those who curse them.

*The fifth step is self-revelation.* **Scripture: Ps 36:5, 105:1, 117:1, 31.5.**

44] The fifth step of humility is that a monk does not conceal from his abbot any evil thoughts entering his heart, or any evils secretly committed by him. Instead he confesses them humbly. 45] Scripture admonishes us about this: "Reveal your way to the Lord and hope in him." 46] Again: "Confess to the Lord, for he is good; his mercy is for ever." 47] And again the Prophet: "I have acknowledged my sin to you; my unrighteous deeds I have not concealed." 48] I said: "Against myself will I denounce my unrighteous deeds to the Lord, and you have forgiven the wickedness of my heart."

*The sixth step is contentment with the least of everything.* **Scripture: Ps 72:22-23.**

49] The sixth step of humility is that a monk is content with all that is little esteemed and with

the least of everything and judges himself a bad
and worthless worker in everything he is given to
do. 50] He says to himself with the Prophet: "I am
brought to nothing. I am ignorant, I am no better
than a beast before you, yet I am always with you.

*The seventh step is a sharp awareness of one's own liabilities.*
*Scripture: Ps 21:7, 87:16, 118:71-73.*

51] The seventh step of humility is that a monk
not only proclaims with his tongue but believes
with the deepest feeling of his heart that he is
inferior to all and more worthless. 52] He humbles
himself and says with the Prophet: "I am a worm
not a human being, one scorned and despised by
people." 53] "I was exalted, then I was humbled
and confused." 54] And again: "It is good for me
that you humbled me so that I may learn your
commandments."

*The eighth step is the avoidance of individualist and attention-seeking*
*behavior.*

55] The eighth step of humility is that a monk does
nothing except what is recommended by the common rule of the monastery and the example of the
elders.

*The ninth step is the radical restraint of speech.* **Scripture:**
**Prov 10:19, Ps 139:12.**

56] The ninth step of humility is that a monk
forbids his tongue to speak, restraining his speech
and not speaking until an answer is required. 57]
Scripture shows this: "In much speaking sin is not

avoided." 58] And: "A talkative person has no direction on earth."

*The tenth step is the avoidance of laughter. Scripture: Sir 21:23.*
59] The tenth step of humility is that the monk is not ready and prompt to laugh, for it is written: "A fool exalts his voice in laughter."

*The eleventh step is gravity in speech. The quotation is not from Scripture, but from the* Sentences *of the philosopher Sextus compiled at the end of second century.*
60] The eleventh step of humility is that when a monk speaks he does so mildly, without laughter, humbly, with gravity and in a few reasonable words. He does not speak in a loud voice. 61] As it is written: "The wise are known for their few words."

*The twelfth step is total humility—in all that is said or done. Scripture: Lk 18:13, Ps 118:107.*
62] The twelfth step of humility is that a monk in his body as well as in his heart always manifests humility to those who see him. 63] This is, at the Work of God, in the oratory, the monastery, the garden, on a journey, in the fields, or anywhere else. Whether he sits, walks or stands, his head is to be always bowed and his eyes fixed on the earth. 64] At every hour, regarding himself as guilty because of his sins, let him consider himself already at the fearful judgment of God. 65] Let him always say in his heart what the publican in the Gospel said, his eye fixed on the earth: "Lord, I am a sinner.

I am not worthy to raise my eyes to heaven." 66]
And with the Prophet: "I am bent over and
humbled in every way."

*At the top of the ladder is the goal of the ascent: perfect love.*
*Scripture: 1 Jn 4:18.*

67] Now, therefore, after ascending all these steps
of humility, the monk will quickly arrive at that
perfect love of God which casts out fear. 68]
Through this love, all that he used to observe
somewhat fearfully, he will now begin to fulfill
without effort, as though naturally, from habit. 69]
[He will act] no longer out of fear of hell, but out
of love for Christ, from good habit itself and delight
in virtue. 70] All this the Lord will by the Holy
Spirit graciously manifest in his workman now
cleansed of vices and sins.

### 3. Why a Ladder of Humility?

St Benedict and his predecessors were attempting to
translate the New Testament exhortation to humility into
behavioral terms. Jesus instructed his disciples to imitate
him in being "meek and gentle of heart". What does this
mean in practice? So the monastic teachers began to
formulate signs or symptoms that the process of conversion
and transformation was underway. The various signs
or indicators were considered to mark stages in the
journey from fear to love. This is why the Master and
Benedict both use the image of the ladder. It is a
traditional monastic way of describing stages of
development. As we grow in Christian life we pass
through different seasons of experience, each having its

particular graces and its distinctive challenges. Humility is necessary at all levels of growth, but its expression is different according to the measure of our progress. As a pastor, Benedict was aware that the field of monastic endeavor broadens in the course of a lifetime. There are always new tricks to learn; an attitude or behavior that may have seemed inappropriate or unattractive at an early stage of development may become important later on. The ladder of humility gives us a sequential account of the way in which humility manifests itself over forty or fifty years of monastic living. There will be personal variations from the general scheme, of course, but the process remains similar for most people.

It is important to remember that this presentation of humility is primarily descriptive and not prescriptive. Benedict nowhere names humility a virtue, that is to say, an habitual disposition which results from the repetition of the appropriate actions. In the context of Cassian's designation of the different forms of humility as manifestations or indicators, the behavioral expressions listed in this chapter are to be seen more as pointers to an inward growth that has already taken place, than as infallible means of achieving it. Humility is an interior quality. Benedict is clearer about this than the Master.[10] He is not proposing a code of manners immediately to be given to newcomers in its entirety. He is offering a description of the normal changes seen at the level of attitude and behavior when a monk continues to go forward. The steps of humility are like milestones on the road towards God. They do not cause progress; they merely measure it. Although external efforts can modify dispositions, it is probably not a good idea to encourage people to practise the

outward forms of humility long before the requisite
changes in attitude have taken place. The outcome of
such premature practice is role-playing and maybe even
hypocrisy. According to St Benedict a monk "should
not wish to be called holy before he is, but first to
become holy so that he may be more truly described as
such" (4.62). The best advice for everyone is to begin at
the beginning and, then, patiently to work one's way
through until the end is attained. In fact, attempting to
be too humble too soon is itself a violation of humility.

The image of the ladder implies movement, and
movement demands a point of origin and a destination.
Is it possible to state, in general terms, where the journey
of humility begins and where it is likely to end? Again it
is helpful to consult Cassian. He has another schema
which locates humility in a broader context.[11]

> Fear of the Lord
> Salvation-bearing compunction
> Renunciation or spiritual nudity
> **Humility**
> Mortification of the movements of the will
> Expulsion of the vices
> Acquisition of the virtues
> Purity of heart
> Perfection of apostolic charity

The beginning of the process is the experience of
conversion, being called by God to a profound change in
outlook and orientation and the willingness of the one called
to leave all things behind, "naked to follow the naked Christ".
The phenomenology of humility which we find in the

monastic sources takes as an initial focus that state of being which follows the act of material renunciation. This is the moment when a decision is made to express practically one's radical determination to follow Christ. For many this coincides with a choice to pursue a monastic life. Without wishing to undervalue the post-baptismal but pre-monastic life of the new monk, it can be said that the first steps of humility are usually associated with the early stages of monastic experience, although some elements may have already been confronted previously.

The foot of the ladder stands at the beginnings of a spiritual life. For St Benedict this leads a man towards entry into monasticism. The process of ascent is conceived as beginning with the experiences encountered in following a vocation. Needless to say every person is different. In some cases, stages precede arrival at the monastery by many years, in others they appear only after years of monastic affiliation.

The start of the process is not so important. Most persons interested enough in the subject to read this book will already have passed through some of the stages that Benedict describes. It is hard to imagine why anyone would want to read a book like this unless they were earnest about the spiritual life! More important for all of us is to know what lies ahead.

It is clear from both John Cassian and Benedict that the final product of humility is perfect love. The end of the monastic process corresponds to the fundamental Gospel teaching on the primacy of love. It also relates to what RB 72 says about love as the soul of all true monastic observance. Even in this life the experience of receiving and giving unconditional love is possible. The ladder of humility does not stretch interminably beyond sight. Its summit is visible. The goal attained by the ascent of humility is one that is accessible if one takes the trouble to use the appropriate means. No wonder Benedict regards his teaching as a way to life (RB Prol 20).

In believing that the goal of perfect charity is attainable in this life Benedict differs from his major source. The Master concludes his treatment of humility with 30 verses which depict the heavenly reward of one who has successfully reached the top of the ladder. After a detailed description that attempts to be lyrical but succeeds only in being quirky, the Master concludes thus.

> This is the celestial homeland of the saints. Blessed are they who can be raised to this enduring region, having climbed the steps of humility through the ladder of observance in this present time. They will rejoice in perpetual jubilation with God. This God has prepared for those who love him and who keep his commandments and are clean of heart. (RM 10.118-122)

By leaving out this long section—perhaps as offensive to his innate sobriety of expression—Benedict places the emphasis on the effects of humility that are verified in this life. Later in this book we will summarize them under two headings: integration and transformation. Here I simply draw attention to the different time scale employed by the two rules. Benedict seems to see humility less as a blind practice that will be duly rewarded in heaven than as a clear-sighted and reasonable sequence of steps that punctuate growth in grace and godliness. It is not a question of theory and supposition, but the result of personal experience and keen powers of observation.

In interpreting the austere teaching of Benedict, it is important to keep in mind what he considers to be the purpose of the whole process. It is growth in love and the transfiguration of the whole personality. This is lofty teaching, and it is worth repeating Benedict's encouragement to the beginner not to be frightened of seemingly impossible demands.

> We are establishing a school of the Lord's service. In this formation we hope not to prescribe anything that is harsh or too heavy. If there is some restriction, it is because reason demands it for the correction of vices and the preservation of love. Do not be frightened by this and desert the way of salvation, because it is narrow only at the beginning. As we make progress in the monastic way of life and in faith, the heart will be enlarged and the way of God's commandments will be run in the extreme sweetness that comes from love. (RB Prol 45-49).

Let us take courage. This difficult chapter may be the means of helping us to come to grips with an important aspect of gospel living that may have hitherto eluded our understanding.

There is a final point that may be made and it is a little sobering. Benedict is clear that although he is describing the stages of ascent, it is also possible to go in the opposite direction. Wherever we are, descent is possible. Bernard of Clairvaux has provided us with a detailed description of the "steps of pride" down which hapless monks might tumble, but this is not the place to discuss this in detail.[12] We simply affirm the possibility.

## 4. Humility in the Context of the Whole Rule

As far as the earlier parts of the Rule are concerned, it seems that Benedict had a tendency to see in the monk's attitude to his abbot the paramount expression of humility. Unlike the Master, Benedict never recommends to the abbot that he be humble or avoid pride and elation. Others raised above the level of the community are so admonished,[13] as are those who receive any sort of preferential treatment (34.4), but not the abbot. The monk proffers his opinion with humility (3.4, 61.4), obeys as an expression of humility (5.1) and knows that his standing in the eyes of the abbot will depend on humility (2.21). It is humility that governs his acknowledgment of faults (27.3, 45.1-2, 57.3). If the community wants to be served by a prior, they must ask humbly (65.14). Guests are to be received in the same spirit (53.6-7, 24). Even love for the abbot is to be tempered by humility (72.10). It seems at first that humility is a one directional attitude, the appropriate stance of a monk before his superiors similar to that required in the presence of earthly potentates or of God (20.1-2).

Most of these instances of humility have an external bearing. Benedict wants his monks to avoid presumption,

elation and anything that would cause them to forget
the fact that their position in the monastery is subordinate. They are not in control. They are obliged to act
in a spirit of submissiveness both to the will of the abbot and to corporate standards and expectations.

Expressed thus baldly, Benedictine humility is not a
very attractive proposition. It seems to make the heart of
monastic living a matter of buckling under an authoritarian
regime. I think that Benedict himself would be a little
surprised at this conclusion.[14] Most of the above texts are
not emphatic, it is only when they are collected and
juxtaposed that they seem oppressive.

The chapter on humility has to be interpreted
within St Benedict's total vision. In reading the text of
RB 7 we need to remember that some of the saint's
attitudes changed as he grew older. The Rule was not
produced in one spurt of composition but slowly
evolved. Progressively, in the later chapters, Benedict
diverged substantially from the Master. Furthermore,
there is evidence that this change of emphasis came from
the fact of St Benedict's exposure to the "Catholic
Fathers". His portrayal of the abbatial function, for
instance, is progressively less severe if we compare the
text taken from RM (RB 2), two chapters influenced by
Cyprian and others (RB 27-28) and a final section that
borrows from Augustine (RB 64). In particular the last
chapters of the Rule reflect a lifetime's experience of
monastic life and some parts even constitute a sort of
retraction of what he had earlier proposed. We can get
a sketchy idea of the development by looking at the
content of these final chapters.

*RB 68 If Brothers are Enjoined Impossible Tasks*

    Benedict recognizes that difficulties in obedience can be objective and not merely the result of immaturity or vice on the part of the subject. He suggests opening channels of communication in case the problem is simply one of misunderstanding the situation from one side or the other.

*RB 69 That in the Monastery None Shall Presume to Defend Another*

    Community life is easily disrupted by inordinate dependence and patronage. St Benedict moves to prevent the kind of relationship that uses kindness as a cloak for subtle domination and the building up on a personal following.

*RB 70 That None Presume to Strike Another*

    Community life is equally disturbed by violence, offi-ciousness and attempting to boss others around. By insisting on clear and unchallenged lines of authority, Benedict set the stage for all to treat one another as brothers.

*RB 71 That Brothers Should Obey One Another*

    Obedience is a benefit to the one who obeys. In practice, obedience is often purest when it is given to those who do not have the power to impose sanctions for its refusal. In a case of conflict of interests Benedict proposes seniority as a means of resolving it.

*RB 72 The Good Zeal that Monks Ought to Have*

    Benedict recognizes that external actions can be ambiguous; much depends on the subjective dispositions which animate them. Therefore he proposes some principles of discern-ment. In the last analysis, however, the value of any course of action is to be determined by the love that it embodies.

### RB 73 That the Observance of All Justice is Not Contained in this Rule

Having come to the end of his work, Benedict recognizes that much has been left unsaid. As a remedy he insists that what he has written be contextualized by reference to the Scriptures and to the writings of the Catholic Fathers and of monastic tradition. Far from seeing his rule as an absolute, as the Master seems sometimes to do, Benedict insists that it is simply a workmanlike handbook to be read only against the backdrop of a wider wisdom.

These chapters are extremely important for the interpretation of the whole Rule. They demonstrate that Benedict was an open and flexible man, one who tried to communicate the fruit of his monastic experience without making it unnecessarily normative. He was willing to learn and to change. He was not proposing a timeless system to be observed literally throughout the centuries but a series of principles which could simultaneously ensure both the stability and the adaptability of the monasticism which bears his name.

Benedict's quality of openness to different values becomes apparent when we notice the dynamic tensions inherent in his presentation. The Rule of Benedict is not an expression of a simplistic ideology. It respects the complexity of the human situation and varied nature of monks' personalities and gifts. As a result the Benedictine monastic institution often seems to be the result of the interplay of different polarities: opposite values working together to produce a harmony. Following are some of these pairs of values.

### Monastic and Ecclesiastical Traditions

Benedict has complemented the psychological and practical wisdom emanating from the Desert Fathers with the more theological insights of the early ecclesiastical writers, many of whom were bishops. Among these Augustine, Basil and Cyprian are particularly important. This duality is apparent in the scheme that Benedict drew up for the Liturgy of the Hours in which elements of traditional monastic usage can be found in combination with contributions from the Cathedral offices.

### Solitary and Community Orientations

The Rule of Benedict has drawn much on a tradition of spirituality that was originally framed for those living as hermits. Yet the way of life described by Benedict is clearly communitarian. The monks pray, eat and sleep together but, on the other hand, there are structures to inhibit interaction, the rule of silence being the most obvious. Another way of highlighting this polarity is to speak in terms of vertical and horizontal. Benedict envisages his monks as being totally drawn towards God but, at the same time, ready to love one another and to live as brothers.

### Abnegation and Humanism

The traditional asceticism of monastic life is not absent from a Benedictine community; the lifestyle is controlled and frugal even though it avoids extremes. Yet, on the other hand, Benedictine monasteries have been traditionally places where the human values are cultivated: a certain refinement, culture, the pursuit of excellence, good taste, an emphasis on quality. The steadfast refusal of many ordinary human gratifications in some sense frees the monk for other equally human gratifications. Perhaps this is part of the "hundredfold" promised in the Gospel.

### Commonality and Personalism

A monastery run according to St Benedict's principles never becomes an institution. Alongside an insistence on the common life, Benedict is careful to advocate personalized attention for every monk. The abbot is "to be at the service of many different temperaments" (2.31) and he is expected to "accommodate and adapt himself to each one's character and intelligence" (2.32), using the skill "of a wise physician" (27.2) and "so arranging everything that the strong have something to yearn for and the weak nothing to flee from" (64.19). "Every age and level of understanding should receive appropriate treatment" (30.1). "The abbot must take their infirmities into account" (48.25, cf. 55.21) and "arrange for help when they need it" (53.20). Artists may use their gifts for the benefit of the monastery so long as their art does not deflect them from their purpose of seeking God (57.1-3). Monks share much in common, but they do not conform to a stereotype.

### *Physical and Spiritual*

The axiom *ora et labora*, popularized in the nineteenth century, expresses an important truth about the form of monasticism that bears Benedict's name. There is a balance between prayer and work, between properly spiritual activities and the ordinary tasks which constitute the daily round, between inner and outer, contemplation and action. The "work of God" is matched by an equal involvement in temporal and physical exertions.

### *Rule and Abbot*

Despite the injunction to maintain his rule in its entirety (64.20, cf. 3.7), Benedict allocates wide discretionary powers to the abbot, saving only that decisions to effect changes are made responsibly and with due deliberation. At first glance Benedict's Rule may seem authoritarian but, in fact, both rule and abbot operate in the context of a particular community so that decisions, more often than not, are the expression of the "common will" rather than impositions from outside or from above.

### *Autonomy and Supervision*

The latent bane of Benedictine monasticism is an innate tendency to degenerate. This has made Benedictine history a history of reforms—presupposing, of course, that the institutions had been seriously in need of corrective action. The most common solution to this problematic tendency is the introduction of yet another polarity: between local autonomy and external supervision. This is only intimated in the Rule (64.3-4). The potential for deviation in a local community can be checked by the institution of a regular visitation designed to identify disruptive tendencies at an early stage and deal with them. This is supplemented by the legislative and judicial functions of general chapters and the support and encouragement that comes from association.

These are polarities in Benedictine life. In most cases Benedict took for granted that the opposed values would somehow work in harmony to produce a synthesis and not result in a fragmented community. In fact he probably expected that all communities would have a little from both sides of the equation, though the proportions would probably prove to be different in each case. One of Benedict's most favored terms is "moderation". He is aware of the dangers of too recklessly pursuing an ideal. Most virtues have an opposite that is equally virtuous. Vice, on the other hand, is frequently the result of a virtue carried to extremes. So Benedict habitually chooses the moderation and discretion of the "Middle Way".

As a result of this internal variety, Benedictine monasticism has demonstrated a remarkable ability to endure. Through many centuries and in different cultures and climates it has had sufficient flexibility to adapt and so to survive. Such a stable institution bears some resemblance to a modern building designed to resist earthquakes. Most of us would assume that the way to construct such a building would be to make everything strong and rigid with lots of concrete and steel reinforcing. In fact, the secret of surviving earthquakes is to have a building which moves with the movement of the earth. Instead of stolidly resisting the tremors, the building sways with them. When the moment is past it flows back into position undamaged. The principles of Benedictine life are solid enough, but there is plenty of room for variety in their expression. As a result, Benedictine monasticism has been able simultaneously to move with the times and retain its own specific character and spirit.

There is a danger in this lack of determination. Instead of respecting both solitary and communitarian values, for instance, it is possible that each is used as an excuse for avoiding the other. In such an unfortunate case, the result is a group of persons who are serious about neither solitude nor community instead of being passionate about both. In other words there is a risk of becoming wishy-washy—an institution without values, committed only to blandness.

When we endeavor to offer an interpretation of the Rule of Benedict we need to be aware of the variety of practical applications that have existed throughout the centuries, each capable of leading monastic men and women to holiness. To speak of humility only in its most extreme expressions is not useful. Such selectiveness voids the reasonableness and wisdom that are Benedict's hallmarks. Humility, above all, needs to be conceived in terms of the breadth of vision which has always been characteristic of the Benedictine tradition at its finest. As we reflect on this theme, we shall try to keep in mind the lessons of history.

## 5. By Way of Bibliography

Following are some titles that are worth exploring, if you want to pursue the meaning of Benedict's seventh chapter. The principal commentaries I have used as back-up and touchstone are the following:

Terrence G. Kardong, *Benedict's Rule: A Translation and Commentary* (Collegeville: Liturgical Press, 1996), pp. 132-168. This is the most comprehensive and (in 1997) the most recent word-by-word commentary available in English. His many articles, listed in the bibliography, on aspects of the Rule are also relevant.

Timothy Fry [ed.] and others, *RB 1980: The Rule of St Benedict in Latin and English with Notes* (Collegeville: Liturgical Press, 1981). This is a gold-mine of historical and critical information. In general I presuppose the abundant material to be found in this volume and do not necessarily repeat it.

Adalbert de Vogüé, *La Règle de saint Benoît* (SChr 181-186 + supplementary volume; Cerf, Paris, 1972-1977). Who dares wins! This is the only 7 volume work available on Benedict's Rule. The chapters on humility are in Vol. I, pp. 472-491 and Vol. VII, pp. 171-183. The latter section is available in English in *The Rule of Saint Benedict: A Doctrinal and Spiritual Commentary*, (CSS 54; Kalamazoo: Cistercian Publications, 1983), pp. 117-126.

Anselmo Lentini, *San Benedetto: La Regola* (Abadia di Montecassino: 1980), pp. 130-165. This commentary gives a clear and sometimes original interpretation of the words and phrases of the Rule.

Georg Holzherr, *Die Benediktsregel: Eine Anleitung zu christlichem Leben* (Zürich: Benziger, 1982), pp. 109-134. I value this work especially for its practical insights.

Here are some articles that cover elements that I touch upon in these reflections. Obviously the list is not complete.

Pedro Max Alexander, "La prohibición de la risa en la Regula Benedicti—Intento de explicación e interpretación," *RBS* 5 (1977), pp. 225-284.

Talal Asad, "On Discipline and Humility in Medieval Christian Monasticism) in *Genealogies of Religion: Discipline and Reasons of Power in Christianity and Islam* (Baltimore, John Hopkins University Press, 1991), pp125-167.

André Borias, "'Primus humilitatis gradus est...' Recherches sur l'herméneutique de Saint Benoît," *RBS* 14/15 (1988), pp. 59-68.

André Borias, "... Saint Benoît nous parle del'humilité," *Lettre de Maredsous* 24 (1995), pp. 4-14, 105-112; 25 (1996), pp. 52-63, 151-164; 26 (1997), pp. 57-69.

Laurence Braceland, "Bernard and Aelred on Humility and Obedience," in John R. Sommer-feldt [ed.] *Erudition at God's Service: Studies in Medieval Cistercian History XI* (CSS 98; Kalamazoo: Cistercian Publications, 1987), pp. 149-160.

Rémi Brague, "L'anthropologie de l'humilité," in *Saint Bernard et la philosophie* (Paris: Presses Univeristaires de France, 1993), pp. 129-152.

Michael Casey, "The Journey from Fear to Love: John Cassian's Road Map" in Pauline.Allen e.a. [ed.], *Prayer and Spirituality in the Early Church* (Everton Park: Centre for Early Christian Studies, 1998), pp. 181-195.

Patrick Catry, "L'humilité, signe de la présence de l'Esprit Saint: Benoît et Grégoire," *COCR* 42 (1980), pp. 301-314.

Joan Chittister, "Humility: The Lost Virtue," in *Wisdom Distilled from the Daily: Living the Rule of St. Benedict Today* (San Francisco: Harper & Row, 1990), pp. 50-66.

Joan Chittister, "Chapter 7: Humility," in *The Rule of Benedict: Insights for the Ages* (New York: Crossroad, 1960, pp. 61-75.

Philip B. Corbett, "Unidentified Source-Material Common to Regula Magistri, Regula Benedicti and Regula IV Patrum," *RBS* 5 (1977), pp. 27-31.

Thomas X. Davis, "Loss of Self in the Degrees of Humility in the Rule of Saint Benedict, Chapter VII," in E. Rozanne Elder [ed.], *Benedictus: Studies in Honor of St Benedict of Nursia* (CSS 67; Cistercian Publications, Kalamazoo, 1981), pp. 23-29.

Benedict Clarkson, "The Rule of Benedict and the Concept of Self-Actualisation," *CSQ* 10 (1975), pp. 22-45.

Placide Deseille, "A propos de l'épilogue du chapitre VII de la Règle," *COCR* 21 (1959), pp. 291-301.

Charles Dumont, "A Phenomenological Approach to Humility: Chapter VII of the Rule of St Benedict," *CSQ* 45 (1985), pp. 283-302.

Denis Farkasfalvy, "St. Bernard's Spirituality and the Benedictine Rule in *The Steps of Humility*," *ASOC* 36 (1980), pp. 248-262.

S. Geisel, "Zum Verbot des Lachens in der Benediktusregel," *Erbe un Auftrag* 67 (1991), pp. 28-34.

Salvatore Giacobbe, "La scala di Giacobbe—L'inter-pretazione ascetica di Gen 28,12 da Filone a San Benedetto," *RBS* 14/15 (1988), pp. 41-58.

André Gozier, "L'échelle de Jacob chez S. Benoît et S. Jean de la Croix," *RBS* 10/11 (1984), pp. 37-44.

Benedict Guevin, "Authenticity: Is this the Meaning of Benedictine Humility? A Response to Antoine Vergote," *ABR* 47 (1996), pp. 225-239.

Odo Hagemeyer, "'Memor quae praecepit Deus' (Regula Benedicti 7,11), *RBS* 12 (1985), pp. 43-48.

Gérard Haverbeque, "L'humilité d'après Saint Benoît," *COCR* 7 (1940), pp. 121-140; 9 (1947), pp. 39-48, 225-230, 317-327; 10 (1948), pp. 173-183, 273-277; 11 (1949), pp. 18-23; 12 (1950), p. 17-25; 13 (1951), pp. 98-107.

Terrence Kardong, "The Fear of the Lord in the Bible and in Benedict's Rule," *Tjurunga* 43 (1992), pp. 25-50.

Terrence Kardong, "Benedict's Use of Cassianic Formulae for Spiritual Progress," *Studia Monastica* 34 (1992), pp. 233-252.

Terrence Kardong, "The Heights of Humility," in *Studia Monastica* 38 (1996), pp. 263-269.

Sighard Kleiner, "Humility," in *Serving God First: Insights on the Rule of St Benedict* (CSS 83; Kalamazoo: Cistercian Publications, 1985), pp. 125-131.

Sighard Kleiner, "Truthfulness," in *In the Unity of the Holy Spirit* (CSS 115; Kalamazoo: Cistercian Publications, 1989), pp. 103-107.

Emmanuel Latteur, "The Twelve Degrees of Humility in St. Benedict's Rule: Still Timely?" *ABR* 40 (1989), pp. 32-51.

André Louf, "Humility and Obedience in Monastic Tradition," *CSQ* 18 (1983), pp. 261-282.

François Masai, "Recherches sur le texte originel du *De humilitate* de Cassien (*Inst.* IV 39) et des Règles du Maître (RM X) et de Benoît (RB VII)" in J.J. O'Meara and B. Naumann [ed.], *Latin Script and Letters* (Fs Ludwig Bieler; Leiden: Brill, 1976), pp. 236-263.

Pierre Miquel, "L'humilité," in *La vie monastique selon saint Benoît* (Paris: Beauchesne, 1979), pp. 104-115.

Matthias Neuman, "Saint Benedict's Teaching on Humility," *Tjurunga* 10 (1977), pp. 61-66.

Andrés Molina Prieto, "Significado de la 'Humilitas' en la espiritualidad benedictina," *Cistercium* 164 (1983), pp. 81-118.

Frumentius Renner, "Die literarische Struktur der Demutsstufen in der Benediktus und Donatus-regel," *RBS* 8/9 (1982), pp. 13-34.

Irven M. Resnick, "'Risus Monasticus': Laughter and Medieval Monastic Culture," *Revue Bénédictine* 97 (1987), pp. 90-100.

Lazare de Seilhac, "Humilitas Christi: A Reading of the Rule of Saint Augustine," *Liturgy OCSO.* 22.3 (1988), pp. 9-23.

Columba Stewart, "The Desert Fathers on Radical Self-Honesty," *Vox Benedictina* 8.1 (1991), pp. 7-53.

Antoine Vergote, "A Psychological Approach to Humility in the Rule of Saint Benedict," *ABR* 39 (1988), pp. 404-429.

Antoine Vergote, "Eclaircissements. A propos d'une lecture du chapitre 7 de l'humilité," *COCR* 46 (1984), pp.75-78.

Ambrose G. Wathen, *Silence: The Meaning of Silence in the Rule of St. Benedict* (CSS 22; Washington: Cistercian Publications, 1973).

Ambrose Wathen, "The Word of Silence: On Silence and Speech in RB," *CSQ* 17 (1982), pp.195-211.

Ralph Wright, "Laughter According to Rose: The Theme of Laughter in *The Name of the Rose*" *ABR* 37 (1986), pp. 396-403.

## Notes

[1] The most complete presentation of the Rule of the Master is by Adalbert de Vogüé, *La Règle du Maître* (SChr 105-107), Cerf, Paris, 1964-65. An English translation has been done by Luke Eberle. *The Rule of the Master* (CSS6; Kalamazoo, Cistercian Publications, 1977).

[2] For an attempt to understand something of the personality of St Benedict as it can be deduced from the text of the Rule see, M. Casey, "*Quod Experimento Didicimus*: The Heuristic Wisdom of Saint Benedict," *Tjurunga* 48 (1995), pp. 3-22

[3] See M. Casey, "The Journey from Fear to Love: John Cassian's Road Map," in Pauline Allen e.a. [ed.], *Prayer and Spirituality in the Early Church* (Everton Park: Centre for Early Christian Studies, 1998).

See also T. Kardong, "Benedict's Use of Cassianic Formulae for Spiritual Progress," *Studia Monastica* 34 (1992), pp. 233-252.

[4] See *Institutes* 4.43; SChr 109, p. 184.

[5] See *Conference* 11.7; SChr 54, p. 105.

[6] See *Conference* 9.2; SChr 54, p. 41.

[7] Apart from the whole first *Conference*, see *Institutes* 12.23; SChr 109, p. 484.

[8] Translated from the Latin in *SChr* 109; pp. 178-180.

[9] References to the Psalms use the Latin (Vulgate) system of numbering, usually one digit lower than the Hebrew system found in most Bibles.

[10] The Master often uses the verb *humiliare* to indicate a bow or reverence; Benedict discontinues this usage. There remains an ambiguity throughout the literature, however, about whether *humilitas* is an objective state of lowliness or humiliation or an inner disposition.

[11] *Institutes* 4.43; *SChr* 109, p. 184.

[12] SBOp 3, 15-59. Icons of St John Climacus also portray the celestial ladder as admitting of two-way traffic. Some monks go up, others fall down.

[13] Thus the prior (65.18), deans (21.5), the cellarer (31.6,13), priests (62.2,5), artisans (57.1-2), those considered competent enough to perform a liturgical function (47.4) and visiting monks whose remarks are to be taken seriously (61.4).

[14] Especially since he seems to associate humility and reasonableness: 31.7, 61.4, 65.14.

# IV
# EXALTATION

**F**ar from being a way of diminishing or dominating persons, humility is a road to freedom, fulfillment and wisdom. This paradoxical outcome can be deduced from the opening verses of St Benedict's chapter. Humility may involve the everyday practice of self-denial, but it is also the means to self-transcendence. This modern word refers to a reality characterized in the Rule by the biblical term "exaltation".

*~1~*

*Brothers, sacred Scripture cries out to us:*
*"All who exalt themselves will be humbled,*
*and those who humble themselves will be exalted."*

Benedict introduces his theme with a saying endowed with scriptural authority. This is a reminder that humility is an integral part of Gospel teaching about how to live. Whatever our feelings about the nature or relevance of humility, the fact remains that it is an inescapable element in the teaching of Christ. As we have already remarked, humility needs to be defined first in spiritual and theological terms and not immediately categorized and judged according to psychological or sociological perspectives.

Humility is the necessary human condition for God's act of exaltation. Because monastic life is totally ordered to our being lifted up by God, humility becomes, for St Benedict, the primary disposition of heart. If we begin from its relation with the action of God we can define humility as the capacity for receiving grace and the gift of final salvation. It is not, in essence, a particular attitude in social dealings but a fundamental stance before God: a willingness to be saved, an openness to God's action, an assent to the mysterious processes by which God's plan is realized in the hearts of human beings. Humility is not an action, nor a sequence of actions, nor a habit formed by the repetition of actions. It is, rather, a receptivity or passivity; a matter of being acted upon by God.

As we reflect on its link with exaltation we become aware that humility is powered primarily by the theological virtues of faith, hope and charity. It is faith that gives us the insight to perceive the workings of Providence in the practical realities of daily life. Hope enables us to endure present incompleteness and negativity in the confident assurance that all things work together unto good. Charity makes us forgetful of self, willing to gives others priority and sincerely seeking God, the ultimate focus of all our loves. It is from this basic Christian attitude of dependence on God that humility springs. In God's plan of salvation all is gift. We have nothing that we have not received from God, no claim to achievement on which to ground any boast.

Here, as elsewhere, we become aware that St Benedict has a very high estimation of the importance of grace in spiritual life. Perhaps this was something that he garnered from his reading of St Augustine or maybe he was protecting himself from the charges that were laid against John Cassian.[1] Because monastic life demands effort, it sometimes happens that monastic authors seem to place too much emphasis on the human contribution to growth in godliness. Many of their writings are directed to inciting the will to make a choice to live well. Grace was taken for granted. The rectitude and effectiveness of the human power of decision seemed more in need of encouragement and support. There is much moral exhortation in monastic texts, but it was never intended to be read outside the context of the inspiration and energy of grace. When we read texts like the Rule of Benedict we need to keep reminding ourselves of their implicit theology of grace.

To picture monastic life as a process of exaltation clearly emphasizes that it is God who is the active agent; the monk is the one who is lifted up. This offsets the impression that the "ladder of humility" is a spiritual Mount Everest that the diligent monk must climb by his own efforts. Self-transcendence is a meaningless concept so long as the self remains in control of the process. Our blind spots are such that not only are we unable to see them, we cannot even perceive our incapacity. We are not aware of which areas in us cry out to be transcended. We need to be acted upon by others.[2] As we have insisted in the last chapter, the behavioral forms of humility are not proposed as a program of exercises to reach the summit. St Benedict offers a description of them as the normal manifestations of growth. Humility is not a state achieved by direct application of effort. It follows the action of God, and is the usual indication that grace is at work.

If we can get it into our heads that humility is to be identified with receptivity of salvation then our reservations about its importance disappear. What St Benedict offers us is an empirical account of the behavioral symptoms indicating that a person is making headway towards salvation.

The primary cause of progress is being willing to receive
the gift, willing also to remove from our hearts and lives
anything that inhibits this receptivity.

In theory, salvation seems desirable. At the level of
feeling it is different. It is humiliating to be saved. You only
have to ask people who have been saved from drowning in
the surf. Often they resist the efforts of their rescuers.
Sometimes they become violent and have to be rendered
unconscious before being brought to safety. To be rescued
is a humiliating experience. Nobody applauds the one who
is saved; the hero is the rescuer. It has been known that
those helped in such circumstances—far from expressing
gratitude—become aggressive or abusive.

The same dynamic bedevils our spiritual life. Many of
us do not want to be helped. We try to do things for
ourselves. We do not want another to save us, whether it be
Christ himself or the Church or a fellow-Christian acting in
Christ's name. We resist what is life-giving because it involves
recognizing that life comes to us from outside and that within
us there is death. The very symbolism of baptism reminds
us that before we assume Christ's life we need to imitate his
humility by going down into the waters to the point of being
submerged. Most of us waste years of our lives trying to
find an alternative way that does not involve this negativity.
We are only prolonging the agony of being unsaved. There
is no alternative. We cannot save ourselves no matter how
creative our imagination. Salvation does not yield itself to
high achievement and sustained effort. We need the
intervention of God to attain our human potential. There
can be no cause for elation here. "That which is exalted
among human beings is an abomination before God" (Lk
16.15).

So many of the images of salvation are images of reversal. God's action means the overturning of the status quo, the relativization of human standards and the breaking of the nexus between cause and effect. The first become last, the hungry are fed, the wilderness blossoms and the parched land is watered. Meanwhile the powerful are unseated, gardens wither and the rich are sent empty away. Divine intervention produces a double effect: those who live in the truth are inundated with life, those that prefer darkness are damned deeper in it.

~2~
*This saying, therefore,*
*demonstrates that all exaltation is a type of pride.*

At first glance this sentiment seems very harsh. St Benedict states as a principle that any form of self-exaltation is an intractable barrier between us and God. There is no use trying to analyze the text philosophically, we need to consult our own experience.

We all would like an easy and prosperous life, but such an existence rarely motivates us to intensify our search for God. When everything is going smoothly, God seems redundant: an abstract and distant deity to whom we give intellectual assent and conventional worship. When we ride the crest of the wave of self-approval it is not hard to forget God. We become practical atheists. Though we may speak of our success in terms of divine blessing, our feeling of well-being is in no way connected with faith, hope and charity. It is the result of lack of difficulties, and a certain confluence of comfort, pleasure, esteem, fulfillment and, above all, the love of others.

Of course, anyone with a few gray hairs can tell us that this happy state will not continue indefinitely. When the inevitable change comes, there is a tendency to mental and spiritual confusion. We blame others. We rage and rail against the supposed perpetrators of our misfortune. It takes much sober reflection to lead us to the conclusion that more often than not we are the real cause of our troubles. Then, maybe we will come to the point where we appreciate that often there is more truth in a situation that is hard, though it is immensely distasteful to admit it.

All this brings us to the point of crisis. Where do we go when we are confronted anew with the paucity of our personal resources? If we try to deny our poverty we beat our heads against the wall of inability, and condemn ourselves to repeated failures. If we completely exhaust our confidence in our capacity to diagnose the situation and to prescribe remedies, then it is just possible that we will look to others for help. This turning to others, if it is sincere and in good faith, will often include the component of trust in God.

So it is that we discover God in hard times. It is the realization of our own limitations that forces us to look beyond human resources for a solution to our discomfort. As Dom Helder Camara notes: "God is far less likely to abandon us in hardship than in times of ease." Saint Ambrose had a similar thought.

> There are many who seek Christ in times of quiet and do not find him. In times of persecution, however, they do find him and find him quickly. The same is true of temptations, since Christ is present to his faithful in dangers.[3]

A text of St Bernard of Clairvaux moves in the same direction. It is the experience of our difficulties that drives us to prayer. When we receive a favorable response then we begin to create from personal experience a picture of God as merciful and kind.

> It is my experience that as long as I keep looking at myself, like Job, my eye is filled with bitterness. But if I look upward and raise my eyes to the help that comes from the divine mercy, then my former bitter vision gives way before the joyful sight of God. Then I say, "My soul is cast down, so I think of you, from the country of Jordan."
>
> Such a vision of God is not to be despised. God is seen as kind and receptive of our prayers, well disposed, merciful and beyond all malice. God's nature is goodness whose special property it is to take pity and to spare.
>
> God is revealed for our salvation through such an experience. It follows this sequence. First of all one perceives oneself to be in dire straits. Then one cries to the Lord and is heard. Then the Lord will say, "I will free you and you shall honor me." So, in this way, self-knowledge is shown to be a step in the direction of knowledge of God.[4]

I am not going so far as to say that we should be happy when troubles come or that gloom should be our constant companion.[5] The simple fact is, however, that it is only when the systems that guarantee normality break down, that we are able to see further prospects.[6] The price of perceiving the possibility of a new and better integration is the disintegration of the status quo. In times of prosperity spirituality stagnates. It is only in the context of the harrowing experience of deconstruction that forward movement is initiated.

Saint Benedict is stating the principle from the opposite vantage point. We do not find God when the going is good. The sense of well-being that is generated by positive experience makes us somewhat self-sufficient. At least it tends to limit our horizons to the range of possibilities available to us in this present world. We become insensitive to other-worldly realities. We forget God.[7] Our experience of life verifies what Benedict says. Elation ("being high") blocks us from God. Being saved is a matter of our being dragged protestingly from our comfort zone to a wild and howling wilderness in which our only security is the faithfulness of God.

Our seeking for certainty elsewhere impedes the action of God. All human-based exaltation is intrinsically false. It cannot be permanent. It postpones our realization that we need God. So it leaves us longer in an unsaved condition. All exaltation is, in fact, a form of pride.

~ 3 ~

*The Prophet shows that he takes precautions*
*against this [kind of pride] by saying:*
*"Lord, my heart is not exalted*
*and my eyes are not uplifted.*
*I have not walked in great affairs,*
*nor in marvels that are beyond me."*

*~ 4 ~*
*For what reason?*
*"If instead of feeling humble, I exalted my soul*
*then, like a weaned child on its mother's lap,*
*you would rebuff my soul."*

This citation of Ps 130 is a little confused. It is a psalm of confidence and trust in God that breathes an atmosphere of simplicity and peace. At first, St Benedict seems to be introducing another image for humility, the image of childlikeness. The words of Jesus on this subject come readily to mind. The attitude necessary to enter the kingdom is that of a small child. There is no place for the blustering autonomy and self-importance associated with making one's way in the world of adulthood.

The second part of the psalm quoted by Benedict is obscure. We do not quite know whether the weaned child is in a relationship of intimacy or rejection. On the one hand the child is on its mother's lap, but on the other it is cut off from its comfort and source of nourishment. It seems that St Benedict understands the relationship as one of rejection.[8] Those who are defective in humility become estranged from God's consolation. Perhaps it is a pedagogical rejection. God wants us to grow out of the immaturity of self-importance and will not have anything to do with us until we abandon pride. Meanwhile we are left hungry and unconsoled. It seems like a hard saying. But there is no doubt in Benedict's mind that without humility spiritual life falters and will eventually be extinguished. By keeping us at a distance, God is training us to a different path.

*~ 5 ~*
*So, brothers,*
*if we wish to attain the summit of the highest humility,*
*and if we desire to arrive quickly*
*at that heavenly exaltation*
*to which we ascend by the humility of this present life,*

*~ 6 ~*
*then a ladder is set up by our ascending actions*
*that Jacob saw in a dream*
*on which there were angels descending and ascending.*

*~7~*
*Without doubt,*
*this descent and ascent is to be understood by us*
*as meaning that we descend by exaltation and ascend by humility.*

*~8~*
*Now the ladder erected is our life on earth,*
*that the Lord will raise to heaven for the humbled heart.*

*~9~*
*We may say that our body and soul are the sides of this ladder,*
*into which God's call*
*has fitted the various steps of humility and discipline*
*by which we must ascend.*

These verses give us the original provenance of the image of the ladder. In Jacob's dream, to which John 1:51 makes allusion, the ladder is that which joins heaven and earth and represents the possibility of two-way traffic, thanks to the mediation of "angels". In subsequent spiritual litera-

ture it was used as a device to illustrate various features
of spiritual progress. Probably the most famous propo-
nent of the imagery was St John Climacus, whose
sobriquet indicates his preference for this perspective.[9]

Benedict's use of the oxymoron "highest summit of
humility" indicates that there is something mysterious and
counter-rational in spirituality. We need to rid our mind
of our obsession with the logic of cause and effect. The
function of this paradox is similar to the use of the koan in
Zen Buddhism. By insisting that we go up only by going
down, Benedict is reminding us that the normal rules of
human behavior do not operate in the spiritual life. We
will understand nothing if we approach the issues from a
"carnal" or "worldly" standpoint. Spiritual matters must
be judged spiritually (1 Cor 2:10-16).

While it is true that God is the principal actor in
spiritual growth, Benedict never underestimates the importance of our contribution. Spirituality and
monasticity are means of entering into eternal life; they
represent a sustained effort to be sensitive and respon-
sive to God's call. It is the lowliness of our present
existence which powers the ascent. Despite the apparent contradiction Benedict is sure of a causal connection
between our practical efforts to avoid raising ourselves
up and our capacity to be lifted by God.

Benedict recognizes that true virtue consists in the
confluence of inner and outer elements. He speaks about
being humble of heart, but also of discipline and appropriate
actions. While priority is given to beliefs, values and
intentions, these interior dispositions and acts lack
effectiveness until they find expression in external behavior.
On the other hand, outward acts have the effect of

reinforcing and intensifying inner attitudes. It is like the chicken and the egg. Logically and ideally interior virtue precedes its outward manifestation. Historically, however, good habits are often acquired simply by being trained in certain ways of behaving. Inner or personal content can be postponed. Values are assumed blindly and carried for years; it is only when some situation arises that calls them into question that they are scrutinized closely. Then they are either internalized or allowed to wane. Rather than trying to establish whether inner disposition or outward behavior has priority, we can follow St Benedict's lead and affirm that both need to be present if progress is to be real. Humility needs both body and soul; it is simultaneously an attitude of soul and bodily behavior.

When we come to examine the sequence of steps which St Benedict describes we will find that Benedict begins with inner dispositions and only very slowly moves towards external behavior.[10] In fact, monastic progress might well be described as the gradual externalization of the secret gifts of grace. The niceties of monastic etiquette have some significance, but they are clearly subservient to the tidal movement of the monk's fundamental assent to the call of God throughout his lifetime.

It is interesting that Benedict links the idea of humility with the notion of *disciplina*. We have to be very careful about translating this word by its English counterpart, "discipline". Discipline often has a harsh and punitive connotation, worthy of a prison or the army. This is one line of meaning that the word has. The other follows from the relation of the word to *discere* and *discipulus*. A discipline is a process of learning. What is required of disciples is that they be willing to learn, that they be teachable, *docibilis* or *docilis*. Unfortunately the English equivalent "docile" is usually taken to mean tame, timid, compliant, submissive, manageable, mouse-like. Discipline is essentially a matter of setting up an external situation that has a capacity to impart knowledge or skills. Docility is the aptitude to profit from such a situation. Benedict understands the monastery as a "school of the Lord's service" (Prol 45). He is aware that it seems restrictive to the newcomer but he expects the way of life to be formative. By participating actively in conventional "monastic" ways of doing things, Benedict anticipates that we will be helped progressively to acquire those interior dispositions which characterize the "real monk".

Benedict assures us that humility will speedily lead us to the goal of our calling. The notion of rapid progress is probably better avoided. Perhaps he meant humility is the most efficient means of growing spiritually. It is certainly not fast. Quite the contrary, experience confirms that humility is a very slow business if it is authentic. A realistic estimate of the time needed to get to the summit would be 40 or 50 years. This is partly because progress is rarely unqualified. In most people's lives there are periods of backsliding, false starts are made, blind alleys entered. Sometimes we go into a loop which stops progress altogether and after ten deluded years or more we find ourselves back where we were. Even if we do not suffer wastage of effort, much time is needed for the restoration of God's image in us. Anyone who zooms up the ladder without let or hindrance is probably going to die young. For the rest of us, it will be a lifelong journey.

Nicodemus was baffled by the idea of being born again (Jn 3:4). Most of us probably feel the same bewilderment and annoyance in hearing about humility. It seems to require the renunciation of our condition as adults responsible for our own lives, and reverting to a situation of childhood, exactly as Jesus taught.

Becoming a child means experiencing our own inability to further the desires that are deepest in us. We discover how resourceless we are, how limited our energies and how fluctuating our will. We cannot survive if we insist on remaining independent. We need help from outside ourselves. Alone we are poor. What seems incredible is that this experience of poverty is the very element that will lead us to open ourselves to the riches with which God intends to endow us.

This is very clear from the background to the chapter given by the psalms. Humility is the special prerogative of the poor, and it is to the poor that salvation is given. Here we see that the monastic approach to humility is very much conditioned by years of using the psalms for prayer. It is, above all, to the lowly and dispossessed that the action of God is directed. No wonder that Jesus begins the Beatitudes by declaring blessed those who are poor.

This blessed poverty is such that it does not admit of limits. It is not only economic or social poverty that is the object of Jesus' praise. All forms of poverty have the effect of making us conscious of our own weakness and lack of resources. Even significant personal failure can have the effect of bringing us to the experience of our own frontiers and motivating us to cross them. Our problems teach us not to rely on ourselves but to learn the freedom that follows our dependence on God. Even our very lack of virtue can expedite our progress towards God. The worse we perceive ourselves, the more likely we are to invest our hopes in the saving intervention of God rather than in our own capacity to find solutions to our difficulties.[11]

People who make a success of the spiritual life are often in grave danger. Their situation is similar to that of the Pharisees in the New Testament. Even religion can become a substitute for God. If we reduce religion to a few good moral habits and some churchly routines, then we are erecting a wall between ourselves and God. God is interested in our hearts not in paltry acts of worship or respectability of life. God wants a relationship, and the only relationship that is authentic is one in which God is the giver and we are receivers. Exactly like small children. They have nothing to give and can do nothing. For what they need to go on living they look to others.

Humility is just one of many Gospel values that poses a lifelong challenge to us all.

## Notes

[1] John Cassian, a contemporary of Augustine, was accused of being a Semi-Pelagian by Prosper of Aquitaine, one of Augustine's disciples. Cassian was antipathetic to Augustine's teachings and expressed himself differently, preferring Eastern sources. So, as far as an unsympathetic reader would be concerned, he left himself liable to the charge that he had not explicitly rejected some of the heresies that Augustine made it his business to refute. His thirteenth *Conference* was especially criticized. To a modern reader, at several removes from the controversies of the day, the charge seems groundless. It stuck sufficiently well, however, to deny the status of sainthood to Cassian in the universal Church. Nevertheless he is venerated at Marseille, and the Eastern Church gives him a qualified approval by celebrating his feast every leap year on 29 February.

[2] When God sets about purifying a human being, the process is accomplished in large measure by human agents. This is because the components of our being which block our receptivity to grace are the very blemishes which other people find ugly. The negative reactions of others serve as a mirror in which we can see reflected those deformations of character against which we need to struggle. The pain we experience in being rejected acts as a purge to motivate us to make ourselves more genuinely lovable. Any advance in this direction has the automatic effect of increasing our openness to the action of God. Of course, one who refuses to acquiesce in the truth of others' reactions becomes more deeply entrenched in bitterness and recrimination and further away from love and God.

[3] *Liber de Isaac et anima* 5, 41; PL 14, 541d-542a.

[4] SC 36.6; SBOp 2. 7-8. Note that "the country of Jordan" was usually interpreted by the Fathers as the land of humility, the name "Jordan" being etymologically connected with the idea of descent.

[5] Quite the contrary. John Cassian included sadness and *deiectio* (downheartedness) among the inner movements of passion which he considered reprehensible. See *Institutes* Book 9: "On the Spirit of Sadness".

[6] "Especially misleading is the fact that the active germination of a growth process often takes place at the low, seemingly negative phase of a psychological cycle." Ira Progoff, *At a Journal Workshop*, Dialogue House, New York, 1982; p. 18. See M. Casey, "The Destruction of Prayer," in *Tjurunga* 51 (1996), pp. 91-102.

[7] As Aleksandr Solzhenitsyn remarked on 10 May 1983 on the occasion of receiving the Templeton Prize for Progress in Religion, "If I were called upon to identify briefly the principal trait of the entire twentieth century, here too, I would be unable to find anything more precise and pithy than to repeat once again, 'Men have forgotten God.' The failings of human consciousness, deprived of its divine dimension, have been a determining factor in all the major crimes of this century." *The Orthodox Monitor* 15 (Jan-July 1983), p. 3.

[8] "Originally, the weaned child was a metaphor for contentment, but now it is a symbol of frustration." Terrence G. Kardong, *Benedict's Rule: A Translation and Commentary* (Collegeville,: Liturgical Press, 1996), p.136.

[9] See the article in the *Dictionnaire de Spiritualité* 4, 62-86: "Échelle spirituelle" by Émile Bertaud and André Rayez.

[10] For some reason St Thomas Aquinas, who had been a boy oblate at Monte Cassino, inverted the order of the steps of humility. See *Summa Theologica* 2-2, 161, 6.

[11] Thus Guerric of Igny, *Sermon for the Saturday of the Second Week of Lent*, 4; SChr 202, p. 36: "If there is anything lacking or imperfect in any of the virtues, humility makes good the defect and makes a profit from the liability."

# V
# SERIOUSNESS

The biblical notion of "fear of the Lord" is not easy to understand and is difficult to market. The updated ritual for Confirmation avoids this by replacing it with "reverence in the presence of God". Such an attitude is certainly part of what is contained within the biblical and monastic concept, but there is more to it than this.[1] I would like to introduce my reflections on the first step of humility with the general heading of "seriousness".

First let me explain what I understand by this term. "Serious" means, among other connotations: deliberate, determined, earnest, genuine, grave, honest, pensive, profound, resolute, sedate, severe, sincere, sober, solemn, stern. This complex sums up many of the elements to be found in fear of the Lord, although the theological content is absent. Seriousness bespeaks a person who is not frivolous. This is to say: not dizzy, empty-headed, flighty, flippant, foolish, giddy, immature, imprudent, incautious, indiscreet, juvenile, light-minded or superficial. This much we can learn from a thesaurus. Perhaps Benedict will have something to add. One thing we know as soon as we begin reading this section is that he believes that to make a beginning in spirituality it is first necessary to take life seriously. Fear of the Lord is the beginning of wisdom, according to a much quoted scriptural aphorism (See Sir 1:11-20). Without a

fundamental earnestness of purpose no progress is possible
on the way to God.

~D~

*The first step of humility
is that a monk always keeps the fear of God before his eyes
and flees from all forgetfulness.*

St Benedict thus serves notice that, in his view, fear of
the Lord constitutes the first and most important element
in all spiritual growth. The most relevant characteristic of
this holy fear is mindfulness, *memoria*, a term with a long
history not only in Christian spirituality but in the traditions
of the great world religions.[2] The opposite disposition is
one of heedlessness, forgetfulness, distraction.

Memory is the opposite of mental numbness, but it is
not necessarily good. The mind also can be corrupt. The
quality of acts of awareness or remembering is defined by
its content. When the memory dwells exclusively on what
individuates, it slows down our instincts towards others, it
alienates and causes loneliness. To the extent that our inner
life is awash with fantasies, we insulate ourselves from reality.
If we remember only what is bitter and hurtful we will always
be unhappy people. On the other hand memory is good
when it helps us to interact with the real world. It is good
when it helps to lessen the shock of the real by interposing
happier thoughts: the mercy of God, the gifts we have
received: our oneness with all creation. The mindfulness
associated with fear of the Lord is good because ultimately
it leads to life.

We begin our ascent with the inner aspect of humility,
not with its outward expressions. Progress in the spiritual

life commences when a person abandons a life built on mindless extroversion or on blind obedience to instincts and unconscious mind-sets. Instead the seeker after God begins to take notice of the promptings of conscience and the first stirrings of spiritual desire. In some cases this awakening coincides with a deep sense of being special in the sight of God, or of being called by God, the primitive intimations of vocation. The question that must be answered is how to respond to such attractions. We may try to ignore them or rebel against them, but often they are too strong to be brushed aside. When we capitulate and allow ourselves to pay attention to these inward leadings, when we let them begin to shape our lives, then we are beginning to be guided by what Benedict calls "fear of the Lord". We are taking the movements of grace seriously.

Often there is a high feeling-content in these initial experiences that constitute what is known as "conversion". A traditional term associated with this was *compunctio* which signaled that the stimulus that leads to our spiritual awakening is often felt as a sting. We are pricked by conscience, by shame at our past, by dissatisfaction with our present, or with an ardent desire for a different future. This feeling is so strong that it is able to overpower our normal lassitude and start us moving in a direction that hitherto we had never seriously explored. A certain amount of drama is necessary to help us make the transition from a comfortable, easy-going and relatively mindless existence to a careful, industrious, zealous and even fervent life. For some, like St Paul, it is a definite, cataclysmic event that results in a definitive change in the direction of their lives. For others it is the accumulation of apparently minor incidents that deftly shepherds them in a particular direction.

And there are those who confront the call in a very low-key manner; it is discernible only by the power it gives them to pursue an unselfish life in a spirit of faith.

No matter how intense the experience of conversion or vocation, it is of the utmost importance that this awakening influence our daily actions. To be true to its nature, the assent given to God in such circumstances needs to become a permanent reality in our ordinary lifestyle. In the language of Latin monasticism, the *conversio* needs to become a *conversatio* (way of life). This is a rule that will accompany us no matter how much progress we make. Whatever we experience spiritually is not merely for our entertainment or encouragement. It needs to become incarnate in our behavior. Otherwise it could well weaken or be lost.

What is extremely difficult to swallow is the absolute nature of the demand. If you read this section of the Rule again, you will notice that it constantly uses terms like "always" and "at every hour". Spiritual life is not a hobby or a part-time occupation. It is nothing if it is does not find expression in everything we do. There is no possibility of moonlighting: using some of our energies for other goals or for ourselves. Taking the spiritual life seriously means that it is not compartmentalized. It is a total obsession. There are no vacations. There are no areas which can be insulated from its guidance. Dabbling in spiritual life is futile; the specific advantages of religious practice follow only when there is unqualified commitment.

Our response to grace is fearful because we recognize our deep affinity with the spiritual world and at the same time we know that we can easily lose grace if we become remiss. Negligence is a great inhibitor of spiritual progress.

It is not that we reverse our fundamental priorities or deny what is important to us. We simply allow ourselves to become absorbed in other activities and the creative tension of life becomes slack. Spiritual realities are unconsciously edged out of our life and allowed to fade. We become "forgetful". It is no longer clear to us that the quality of our routine activities has any bearing on our ultimate fulfillment.

~11~

*He must always remember all God's instructions.*
*The monk is always to turn over in his mind*
*how all who despise God will fall into hell for their sins,*
*as well as the everlasting life prepared for those who fear God.*

The monk's mindfulness has for its content the positive commandments of God, the punishments in store for those who despise God by ignoring them, and the rewards prepared for those who are diligent in fulfilling their obligations. One of the best ways of appreciating what Benedict is saying is to turn to the book of Deuteronomy. The whole purpose of this prophetic restatement of Mosaic law was to encourage the people to remember all that God had spoken, to carry it in their hearts and implement it in their lives. The message is proclaimed by the Deuteronomist in both promises and threats. The carrot and the stick. Exactly as Benedict does. It may be that as the monk develops he will act from more gratuitous and disinterested motives. At the end of this chapter Benedict gives us a picture of a monk who has been liberated from every sense of compulsion and acts only out of love. But there is no harm in reminding the beginner of the dire seriousness of free will. It is possible to make self-destructive choices.

Anybody with experience of life knows this. A person who does not feel dread in situations which involve irreversible decisions is a fool. Freedom is an awesome responsibility. It allows us to determine our own fate even though we cannot know in advance the ultimate significance of the possibilities that confront us.

The definitive manifestation of such life-denying choices will be at the final judgment. There we will be nakedly exposed in the state we ourselves have brought about. It will be a time of truth. There will be no scope for a barrage of excuses to cover our condition. We will have no alternative but to take responsibility for what we have made ourselves and allowed ourselves to become. It may be that we do not much like the concept of the Last Judgment. The fact remains that it is one that is thoroughly entrenched in the Gospels and in the New Testament and the Creeds. It may not have always had the dramatic imagery with which the medievals endowed it. This truth of faith cannot be ignored simply because we feel that it would be nicer if God did not judge. Either this is true or the whole Christian vision is suspect. Judgment is not an optional extra. We have to try to come to an understanding of how it fits into Gospel living. It may be that when all else fails to motivate us to turn away from evil and do good, the realization of our future accountability will serve to jolt us from a course of action that is unworthy of us, or help us to make the effort to go beyond ourselves to be of service to others. It is in this sense that Benedict reminds the monk who reneges on his commitment that he will be condemned as one who mocks God (RB 58.18).

There is not much about the theme of *memento mori* (keep death in mind) in the Rule of Benedict. He skips over the prospect of death in the present chapter though it is implicit in that of judgment. It is only in RB 4.47 that the idea surfaces in the context of a series of aphorisms which parallel the present chapter (RB 4.44-54). The focus is entirely on the action of God as the ultimate assessor of the quality of human behavior. The macabre imagery of the medieval "dance of death" is absent from the Rule.

The judgment of God is also an act of salvation. It is not only the rejection of those who have rejected God. It is the means by which those who have desired and sought God in this life are definitively united with the object of their search. The doctrine of the final judgment should really be a comforting one. In this life the goodness that we attempt is not always understood, appreciated or accepted. Sometimes we are peppered with blame even when we know we have acted with integrity. The judgment of God will be the occasion in which the truth will become evident to all. If our lives have been noble and beautiful, then this will be the moment of ultimate vindication.

~12~
*Let him guard himself at every hour*
*from sins and vices,*
*be they of thought or tongue, of hand or foot,*
*of self-will or fleshly desire.*

To some extent the whole program of Christian life is summed up in the verse of Psalm 33 which Benedict quotes in the Prologue: "Turn away from evil and do good." The important word is "and". Spiritual warfare is two-pronged: it both attacks and defends. We must be active in the performance of good works and at the same time recognize and struggle against whatever detracts from the beauty of our admirable deeds. To some extent it is easy enough to avoid evil by doing nothing; living a marginal life, keeping out of trouble and investing all our energies in private pursuits. And it is not difficult to do good if we have no objection to mixing ambition and selfishness in our benefactions. Simultaneously to do good and eschew evil is always a challenge.

Benedict decides to place the initial emphasis on dealing with sin. This is due to the specific situation that the Rule addresses. By entering a monastery, the neophyte commits himself to a sizable chunk of good works each day. Simply by giving himself to the monastic ethos the monk lays down a positive foundation in Christian living. Benedict, however, recognizes that material performance is of no avail if it is not accompanied by the corresponding internal dispositions. In Chapter 72, for example, he contrasts "good zeal" and the "zeal of bitterness". It is the quality of interior attitude that gives the moral specificity to the monk's actions. Once a certain level of good living is established it is time to look to the opposite pole of the dialectic and begin taking steps to uproot sin. Benedict is presupposing some progress in virtue before the campaign against vice begins.

Like many of the ancient writers Benedict is not surprised to find vices latent in the heart of the monk. Their presence is not morally reprehensible except in so far as someone has neglected to struggle against them. His presupposition is that any man coming to a monastery will have all the vices within him. In the course of a lifetime these will manifest themselves in a variety of temptations and crises. These outbreaks will give the monk the opportunity to resist his evil tendencies. When, by grace, they are overcome the monk goes forward somewhat lighter, he is no longer burdened by their hidden weight. His heart is less divided, his energies less dispersed. On the other hand, someone who is never tempted and has never passed through a crisis is probably crippled interiorly by the presence of undiagnosed and, therefore, unresisted vices and tendencies. There is no overt sin but simply a mysterious inner heaviness that dulls enthusiasm and blocks contemplation. The image that Cassian uses is that of a feather that has been wet. It is no longer light enough to be carried aloft by the faintest breeze. In defiance of its natural tendency, it simply drops to the ground. We do not rid ourselves of the sluggishness of sin simply by keeping out of trouble. We have to identify our vices and eliminate them. The Desert Fathers used to say that the principal occupation of monasticism is the struggle against "demons".[3] Part of the truth of Benedictine life is that it leads the monk or nun to a point where the measure of innate sinfulness may be calmly recognized so that it can be systematically reduced.

Nowadays we have an opposite tendency. We assume that only bad people have evil tendencies. We tend to regard children as innocent and novices as no-vices. Any sort of eruption in later life we regard as a sign of backsliding and we often reproach people for not being as good as they used to be. In fact we can be reasonably certain that whatever surfaces has already been latent for years. When difficulties arise it means that they have at last entered the realm of consciousness. Finally they demand a response from us at the level of understanding and will. It is really cause for congratulation. Yes, we face an uncomfortable struggle. But with God's help it is not unwinnable.

Humility constantly confronts us with our moral fragility and keeps reminding us that we need to do battle if we are to remain upright. It is a sobering attitude that will not allow us to deal with our liabilities by a perfunctory dismissal. This is why the ancient monks used the imagery of spiritual warfare. Christian life is a struggle. "Let those who stand take heed lest they fall" (1 Cor 10:12).

"Vigilance is the price of liberty," according to the motto adopted by NATO. A country at war increases its watchfulness, especially at its frontiers. It seeks to put into operation a 24-hour early warning system that will enable its forces to regroup in response to any oncoming danger. This is what Benedict is recommending to his monks, following a tradition of psychological expertise that draws on the Desert Fathers, Evagrius Pontikus and John Cassian. We need to understand the mechanics of temptation and sin so that we can intervene in the process and stop the inevitable threat to our integrity. Fear of the Lord concerns the prevention of sneak attacks that allow our evil tendencies to seize control in a moment of weariness or inattention. Otherwise it will be as though the soul's immune system has been dismantled. The will and the capacity to resist will have been rendered ineffectual and we will inevitably become slaves.

Fear of the Lord is the first line of defense against all kinds of vices. Benedict thinks in terms of overt sins of thought, word and action. To these he adds self-will, a more hidden vein of ugliness, since it often conceals itself behind actions that are otherwise laudable. Self-will poisons whatever it touches. It is a far more fundamental deformation than merely thinking, saying or doing what is wrong. Even more primal than self-will are those sub-personal inclinations that are accompanied by strong feelings and seem to have their base in the physical organism. Benedict calls them "the desires of the flesh"; they are often referred to as "the passions". Lust is one of them, but there are many more. We will have more to say on this subject when it comes to the second step of humility. What is important for the moment is the thought that the basic role of "fear of the Lord" is defense against our innate contrary tendencies. Expressed more positively, being serious about our spiritual life is necessary for the safeguarding of the integrity of our personal freedom.

~13~
*Let the monk consider*
*that at every hour human beings are always seen*
*by God in heaven, that their actions in every place*
*are in God's sight and are reported by angels at every hour.*

~14~
*The Prophet demonstrates this to us*
*when he shows that God is always present in our thoughts:*
*"God searches hearts and kidneys."*

~15~
*Again he says:*
*"The Lord knows the thoughts of human beings."*

~16~
*And in the same vein:*
*"You understand my thoughts from afar."*

*~17~*
*And:*
*"Human thought will be open before you."*

*~18~*
*That he may be careful about his perverse thoughts,*
*the good brother should always say in his heart:*
*"I shall be blameless before God*
*if I guard myself from my wickedness."*

Benedict does not expect the truth of God's surveillance to be self-evident. The monk needs to reflect on the matter in the light of scriptural teaching. God sees not only our external actions but is able to scan our innermost motivations. In biblical terminology the heart was the seat of the higher intellective functions; gut-feelings and emotions were located in the kidneys. Whatever facade we maintain, the gaze of God penetrates the inner chambers of our personality. We find the theme developed in the Wisdom books of the Old Testament:

> The eyes of the Lord are ten thousand times brighter than the sun, they look on every aspect of human behavior... Nothing is better than fear of the Lord and nothing is sweeter than to heed the Lord's commandments. (Sir 23:19,27.)

Reversing the terminology we might say that we remain in the active mind of God. All human beings are present to God by virtue of creation. This is what having existence means. Nothing that we do, say or think escapes the notice of God; every act has eternal significance and eternal consequences. Benedict reinforces his point with another graphic image. Our external acts are constantly reported to God by his angels: his information on us is being constantly updated.

Benedict has inherited from the Master a fairly primitive angelology. Of the 17 references in RM he has kept only five: the description of Jacob's ladder (7.6), two references to the angels as reporters of our conduct to God (7.13, 7.28) and two allusions to the idea of the angels being present during the liturgy (19.5, 19.6). According to ancient standards this is a fairly sober presentation.[4] Benedict took all these texts from his principal source as a convenient way of describing the divine awareness of human behavior. But he does so with no particular emphasis.

Benedict, following the Master, supports his assertion that God knows our thoughts with a barrage of texts from the Old Testament. In an organized and somewhat controlled society such as a monastery there are many rules and conventions about conduct and conver-sation. The only way that a monk can indulge in aberrant or subversive activity is in the privacy of his own cell or in the secret enclave of his imagination. The institution of patrolling circatores, who kept an eye on observance, was designed to deal with the first possibility.[5] The second eludes human policing. So Benedict, knowing that alternative thoughts eventually generate deviant actions, submits them to divine sanction.

A more benign reading of the text would find in it evidence of Benedict's concern that there be a consistency between the outward actions which a monks performs and the inner world of his imagination. It is not merely the foolish desire for total domination that we see typified in the so-called "Thought Police" of George Orwell's *1984*.

From monastic tradition Benedict knew the importance of
working with one's spontaneous thoughts as a means of
assessing one's spiritual status and exercising some measure
of self-determination. Unexamined thoughts have too much
power. If one is to remain free, then one needs to break the
automatic connection between thoughts, feelings and action.
To submit one's impulses to discernment. To make a choice
of what inclinations will be expressed by outward deeds.

Verse 18 sums up St Benedict's view of fear of the
Lord as mindfulness. Even a good monk has thoughts that
go in a direction opposite to that of his profession.[6] These
are not to be repressed or denied, but frankly admitted. If
the monk sets himself the task of ensuring that these inner
eruptions do not find expression in his conduct then he can
relax in the knowledge that God will adjudge him blameless.

~19~
*Indeed, we are forbidden to do our own will,*
*when Scripture says:*
*"Turn away from your willfulness."*

~20~
*Again, in the [Lord's] Prayer, we ask God*
*that his will be done in us.*

~ 21 ~
*We are rightly taught not to do our own will,*
*since we should beware of what Scripture says:*
*"There are ways which seem humanly right*
*whose end plunges into the depths of hell."*

These three verses take up the matter to be treated in the second step of humility, the doing of God's will. It will be impossible for us to embrace God's will if we are inordinately attached to our own way of viewing reality: our experiences and memories, our powers of judgment, the independence of our assessment. Self-will is sometimes willful rebellion and sometimes mere cussedness. More often it is a matter of mind. If we have allowed the integrity of our mind to become impaired through abuse, we will find ourselves locked into a partial perspective of reality. There will be a strong tendency to concentrate on one segment of the available data and arrive at conclusions and make judgments on this basis. We may be emotionally committed to the resultant view, but here, as elsewhere, the objective credibility of an opinion is in no way related to the intensity of feeling with which the opinion is held. So what is termed self-will is not always a problem of will. Mostly it is a closed mind and that is the result of not being simultaneously open to conscience, the Word of God and those whom Providence has given us as our guides in the faith.

As the opposite of pride, humility is the mortal enemy of all rebellion against God. It is, in part, a willing acceptance of divine authority. To be subject to God first we need to recognize that all our desires are to be submitted to intelligent assessment before being followed. We have to declare our independence from their automatic governance. Secondly, we need to develop in ourselves a real desire for the coming of God's kingdom. If it is with sincerity that we pray "Thy will be done" then, in times of difficulty, it will be easier to adopt the prayer of Jesus in Gethsemane, "Not as I will, but as you will". This requires a robust faith and a practical acceptance that the will of God is always to our benefit, even though hopes are dashed and feelings affronted. Humility demands that we acknowledge our incapacity to perceive the total picture. In the course of a lifetime there will be many incidents which we will retrospectively evaluate as special favors from God which, at the time, seemed incompatible with fatherly concern.

Benedict's citation of Proverbs 16:25 is meant to plant a few seeds of doubt about the wisdom and ultimate value of following the spontaneous promptings of our lower nature. The Master has changed the originally singular "way" into the plural to make the text into a plea for everyday discernment. Benedict follows him in this. See also RB 3.13, addressed to the abbot: "Do all things with counsel and you will not be sorry afterwards" (Sir 32:24). The point is clear enough. Good will is not always sufficient to ensure the profitability of a venture. We need to take precautions against being led astray by our own inexperience. We can issue rosy press releases about what we are doing and win the approval of all. We can change public opinion. We can wheedle the necessary permissions. But we cannot change the nature of reality. Like the Emperor with no clothes we can be insouciantly unaware of the intrinsic quality and significance of what we do. It is hard to make a reproach stick. But a course of action that is foolish or destructive does not become less negative because we are ignorant of its dangers. It just means that we are caught by surprise when the true nature of what we have been advocating is revealed. It is like our attachment to suntans, tobacco or fatty foods. The fact that we believe that they are harmless makes no difference to their effect on our bodies. Reality has the habit of imposing its will on us, whether we care to acknowledge its existence or not. The more stupid we are, the longer it takes for the truth to dawn on us.

~ 22 ~
*In addition, we are afraid of what is said*
*about the negligent:*
*"They have been corrupted*
*and have become disgusting in what they choose."*

~23~
*Let us believe that God is always present to us*
*even in the desires of the flesh*
*for, as the Prophet says to the Lord:*
*"All my desire is before you."*

~24~
*We must, then, beware of evil desire,*
*because death stands near the entrance of delight.*

~25~
*For this reason Scripture instructs us:*
*"Do not pursue your lusts."*

In verse 22 we see the first appearance in this chapter of what we may term "psychological fear". In fact this is the only use of the verb *pavere* in RB or RM.[7] What must we fear? We become frightened when we think of how easy it is for the spiritual life to be destroyed by mere mindlessness. If we appreciated the insidious power of negligence to bring our hopes to nothing, we would certainly be motivated to be diligent in keeping watch over the quality of daily behavior. If we know a road we drive on is dangerous, we instinctively slow down and keep our wits about us. This is what Benedict is recommending. We should be a little frightened at the power of our fragility to wreak havoc on what we cherish most.

First Benedict spoke about thoughts and then about self-will. Now he changes the focus to address the underlying energies which power so many thoughts and schemes. "The wish is the mother of the thought" according to the ancient aphorism. So Benedict implies that relief from intrusive thoughts will only come when the monk has done something about the instinctual desires which are their wellspring.

He relates the subduing of such desires with godly fear and mindfulness, by alerting us to the dangers of negligence. Most people are not positively malign. If they succeed in getting their lives into a mess it is usually because they have let things slip "on a temporary basis". There was no dramatic change of direction, just a gradual slowing down and an imperceptible loss of focus. So Benedict tells us to be careful. What began as harmless relaxation eventually leads to a substantial decline in the quality of life. At some point change for the worse takes place. Perhaps there is no dramatic act of will, just the cumulative effect of unrelieved self-centredness, that eventually robs a life of any objective beyond itself. Of course, one of the things that locks the process of decline into inevitability is our defensiveness and rationalization. We so readily convince ourselves that we are blameless that neither the impact of reality nor wise counsel can shake our sureness. We are convinced that if there is a problem then the fault lies with others.

Here Benedict's circular method of presentation becomes evident. Following the Master's lead he has a little more to say on the matter of carnal desires. It is not mere repetition. He now speaks about evil desires and uses the technical word "concupiscence", which often refers especially to sexual desire.[8]

The phrasing of verse 23 is interesting: God is no stranger to our carnal desires. I prefer a literal translation here and in verse 14, whereas Terrence Kardong inverts the imagery: "God is always privy to our thoughts...our lower inclinations are well known to God".[9] If God is present, there is no excuse for denial. "We are told that Catherine of Siena once cried out: 'My God and Lord, where were you when my heart was plunged in darkness and filth?' And she heard the answer: 'My daughter, did you not feel it? I was in your heart.'"[10] This seems to signify that even instinctual cravings and their physical expression are not a domain exclusive to the devil and solely under his or her influence.[11] Somehow God is present even in these violent and intensely individual outbreaks that most dramatically signal our rebellion. Temptations having their origin in carnal desires cannot be indulged as irresistible. Beneath the tumult God is present. Inevitability follows only when the monk refuses to join battle, or in weariness does not pursue it to the end. God is there to be discovered even in the act of prolonging resistance to temptation.

The danger inherent in temptation is that it weakens our desire to find delectation in God and offers us more accessible and less costly substitutes. "Their belly is their God" (Phil 3:19; cf. Rom 16:18). "Avarice is the service of idols" (Col 3:5). The word used in RB is *delectatio*. Not *voluptas*, *libido*, *oblectatio* or the related word in the plural *deliciae*. All of these would emphasize the fleshly content of hedonistic experience. *Delectatio* has a wider meaning; as well as bodily pleasure it can easily refer to spiritual or personal enjoyment. The danger of sinful pleasure is not that it is pleasurable, but that it undermines the search for more enduring delights. And because it is a stand-in for something else, it proves inadequate. It often leaves a sour aftertaste which then has to be chased by further indulgence. The ascetic side of monastic life involves the sacrifice of many ordinary pleasures. This is not because there is something wrong with simple joys. The problem is that a certain starvation at the level of physical gratification enhances the sensitivity of the monk to spiritual delights. Just as wine-tasters need to keep their palates clean for their task, the monk needs to avoid seeking substitutes for finding his joy in God. Without some restriction of pleasure he will make little progress in his chosen avocation.

St Benedict is saying that as soon as any pleasure becomes a priority the vitality of our monastic commitment is eroded. He illustrates this first with a passage from Pseudo-Ambrose's account of the martyrdom of St Sebastian. It is another reminder of how much early "monastic" spirituality is indebted to the literature about the martyrs.[12]

> Those who in this mortal life fight against their lusts and against *delectatio* and do not give into them will, in the future, receive them in their entirety from their Creator. For God created the human being to

have life and he placed death near the entrance of delight so that those who wish to escape the fear of death may seek eternal life.[13]

Exactly what the text originally meant by this juxtaposition of death and delight is not completely certain. Perhaps there is a reference to the Seraphim barring the entrance to Eden, the garden of delights. Who knows? For the Master and Benedict, however, the point they are making is clear. Spiritual life is incompatible with the pursuit of pleasure. This is confirmed by the citation of Ben Sirach: "Do not pursue your lusts." Sometimes, however, it seems rather that our lusts pursue us.

~26~
*Therefore, because the eyes of the Lord*
*are watching the good and the wicked,*

~27~
*and because the Lord is always looking down from heaven*
*on human beings*
*to see whether any understand and seek God;*

~28~
*and because every day, day and night,*
*the angels assigned to us report our doings to the Lord,*

~29~
*then, brothers, we must beware at every hour*
*or, as the Prophet says in the Psalm,*
*"God may, at one time, see us falling into evil*
*and become useless."*

*~ 30 ~*
*God spares us at this time because he is kind*
*and waits for us to be converted to something better.*
*In the future, he may say to us:*
*"You did this, and I was silent."*

These verses serve as a recapitulation of Benedict's teaching on fear of the Lord. God is watching us, his angels report on our conduct. Therefore constant vigilance is necessary. Otherwise we will become worthless, *inutiles*—a radical enough word for someone as pragmatic and Roman as Benedict. But we have a chance to amend, God has given us the possibility. He has extended the deadline. If we let the opportunity slip past us we will have only ourselves to blame. The time to start taking life seriously is now.

It is a sober view of reality, one that probably recommends itself more to persons of mature years and some experience. There is truth in what Benedict is saying. If we find ourselves inclined to set it aside, then perhaps the problem is ours, not Benedict's. He is, in fact, doing no more than affirming that the responsibility for the quality of our lives remains with us. He is expressing this in terms derived from a long experiential tradition, already well developed by the time of Antony of Egypt.

> [Abba Antony] also said, "Always have the fear of God before your eyes. Remember him who gives life and death. Hate the world and all that is in it. Hate all peace that comes from the flesh. Renounce this life, so that you may be alive to God. Remember what you have promised God, for it will be

required of you on the day of judgment. Suffer
hunger, thirst, nakedness, be watchful and
sorrowful; weep, and groan in your heart; test
yourselves, to see if you are worthy of God;
despise the flesh, so that you may preserve your
souls."[14]

## Notes

[1] See Terrence Kardong, "The Biblical Roots of Benedict's Teaching on Fear of the Lord," *Tjurunga* 43 (1992), pp. 25-50.

[2] I have discussed this theme in "Mindfulness of God in the Monastic Tradition," *CSQ* 17.2 (1982), p. 111-126. Reprinted in *The Undivided Heart: The Western Approach to Contemplation* (Petersham: St Bede's Publications, 1994), pp. 61-77.

[3] The same conception appears in Benedict's Rule 1.4; See also RM 1.4.

[4] See Jean Daniélou, *The Angels and their Mission: According to the Fathers of the Church* (Westminster: The Newman Press, 1957). On the other hand, Benedict has five references to the devil, four times in connection with temptation (Prol 28, 1.4, 54.4, 58.28) and once linked with the "world" (53.5). By contrast the Master has one use each of Satan and "demonic" and 39 other references to the devil. It is clear that, once again, Benedict has toned down the Master's dramatic imagination.

[5] See RB 48.17-18. For a general history of this institution see Hugh Feiss, O.S.B., "*Circatores*: From Benedict of Nursia to Humbert of Romans," *ABR* 40.4 (1989), pp. 346-379.

[6] Aldous Huxley termed this contrariety "induction" and stated as a universal law that each decision is followed by strong attractions in the opposite direction. See *The Devils of Loudun*, (Harmondsworth: Penguin Books, 1971, pp. 188-189). "Every

positive begets its corresponding negative. The sight of something red is followed by a green after-image. The opposite muscle groups involved in any action automatically bring one another into play. And on a higher level we find such things as a hatred that accompanies love, a derision begotten by respect and awe...(Every collection of spiritual letters abounds in references to those frightful temptations against the faith and against chastity, to which seekers after perfection are peculiarly subject. Good directors point out that such temptations are a normal and almost inevitable feature of the spiritual life and must not be permitted to cause undue distress.)"

[7] The noun *pavor* appears in RB Prologue 48: "Do not be daunted immediately by fear and run away from the road that leads to salvation." This has no parallel in RM. In this text *pavor* is something to be overcome or avoided; it is not recommended.

[8] Here we need to recognize a distinction between ascetical or moral use of *concupiscentia* and its meaning in dogmatic theology. On the latter see Karl Rahner, "The Theological Concept of Concupiscentia," in *Theological Investigations Volume One*, (London: Darton, Longman and Todd, 1965), pp. 345-382. Also, J. P. Kenny, "The Problem of Concupiscence: A Recent Theory of Professor Karl Rahner," *Australasian Catholic Record* 29 (1952), pp. 290-304 and 30 (1953), pp. 23-32.

[9] *Benedict's Rule*, pp. 132-133.

[10] Thus Jürgen Moltmann, *Jesus Christ for Today's World* (London: SCM Press, 1994), p. 46.

[11] This is a departure from earlier teaching, especially in Jewish Christian circles and later in Evagrius Pontikus, which seemed to presuppose the identification of demons and vices. The vices were thus hypostasized as demons active within the human psyche. Speaking of Origen, Peter Brown writes: "Consent to evil thoughts, many of which were occasioned, in the first instance, by the dull creakings of the body —by its need for food and its organic "sexual" drives —implied a decision to collaborate with other invisible spirits, the demons, whose pervasive presence, close to the human person, was registered in the 'heart' in the form of inappropriate images, fantasies and obsessions. For these

demonic promptings also had a dynamism that could not be explained by the normal stream of conscious thought." See *The Body and Society: Men, Woman and Sexual Renunciation in Early Christianity* (London: Faber and Faber, 1989), p. 167.) The West tended to move away from this assumption, although there is a certain continuity in image and language.

[12] "Monasticism grew out of the most devout circles of the second- and third-century Church, and was strongly marked with the imprint of the spirituality of martyrdom." Thus Claude Peifer in *RB 1980*, Appendix 2, p. 361.

[13] *Acta S. Sebastiani* 4.14; *PL* 17. 1119b. The previous section of this chapter (#13) is quoted extensively by the Master in the evocation of the delights of heavenly existence. Benedict, as we have already noted, omitted the eschatological finale to the Chapter on humility.

[14] Translated by Benedicta Ward in *The Sayings of the Desert Fathers: The Alphabetical Collection* (CSS 59; Kalamazoo: Cistercian Publications, 1975), pp. 6-7.

# VI
# Doing God's Will

The chief effect of fear of the Lord is to break the monk's addiction to self-will and open him to an authentic receptivity of God. He is already saved to the extent that he has been liberated from the destructive power of an unredeemed self. The void thus created calls out to be filled by God's mercy. If this process continues, St Benedict envisages that it will reveal its energy in a greater adhesion to the will of God. Christian obedience is more than buckling under an authoritarian regime—be it ever so sanctified. The Gospels remind us often enough that obedience is the concrete expression of filiation. Following the example of Christ, the monk demonstrates that he is God's son by obeying. Obedience is the foundation of a richer relationship. In a state of disobedience no intimacy is possible. To express the same truth more positively, the medieval mystics remind us that it is conformity to the will of God that leads, after many humdrum years, to our transformation. What begins as obedience ends in our being possessed by love in the experience of contemplation.

The second and third steps of humility cover some of this ground. Inevitably, as we have come to expect in the Rule, there is a certain amount of repetition and overlap. No matter. It enables Benedict to approach the same question from slightly different angles.

~ *31* ~
*The second step of humility is*
*that a monk does not love his own will*
*or delight in the satisfaction of his desires.*

Note, first of all, that at this second step, the doing of God's will does not explicitly involve obedience in the sense of submitting to and conforming with an external command, be it of the law or of those in authority. The initial means of doing the will of God is unseating alternative powers. This means, above all, countering the pervading influence of the passions on our conduct.

Again we see the double thrust of Benedict's teaching. Progress depends both on rejecting sin and embracing goodness. We remember the text of Romans 13:13-14 which was instrumental in the conversion of St Augustine. "Let us conduct ourselves decently as in daytime: not in reveling and drunkenness, not in debauchery and permissive behavior, not in fighting and jealousy. Instead, put on the Lord Jesus Christ and make no provision for the flesh to satisfy its demands." Positive attachment to Christ necessitates a corresponding detachment from those sub-personal forces which hold us in bondage.

The question that each one of us needs to ask is this: Who is my master? Since it impossible to serve two masters, my life needs either to submit to God or consciously to reject divine control and aim at some specious "autonomy". Either I look for self-transcendence based on faith, or I lock myself within my narrow world of experience, memory and perception. There is no possibility of sitting on the fence for more than a brief interval. A choice has to be made that involves the elimination of one option. The kind of commitment called for by our Christian profession does not permit the wearing of a parachute.

Much of the Epistle to the Romans concerns the "obedience of faith" (1:5, 16:26). St Paul notes that this obedience requires of us that we be quit of sin. Thus he says in 6:16-18:

> Do you not know that when you present yourselves to someone as slaves for obedience, you are the slaves of the one whom you obey? Whether it be sin, resulting in death or obedience, resulting in righteousness. Thanks be to God, though you used to be slaves of sin you became obedient from the heart to that form of teaching to which you were committed. Once you were freed from sin you then became slaves of righteousness.

For St Paul, freedom seems to consist less in self-determination than in submission to that power which is objectively higher, more powerful and more beneficent. In such a context the notion of "freedom" to commit sin becomes an absurdity. All wrongdoing is enslavement, the only way to be free is to distance ourselves from sin.

The desire for autonomy and the resistance to all "heteronomy" (as its opposite is termed) leads many people into delusion. To maintain a claim of self-determination many necessities have to be declared irrelevant or denied. This is patently foolish. The laws of physics and biology are never suspended in our favor. We are always subject to them. Our genetic complexion was established without any consultation. We have to eat, drink and rest. We cannot fly. Social scientists likewise insist that we are products of our upbringing. The only way we can escape conditioning is to become aware of its determining power and then consciously to counter it. Denial leads us deeper into thralldom. If autonomy is our goal, we must be aware that it can exist only on a very narrow band within the spectrum of human experience. We are social beings, and community begets interdependence. We sacrifice a measure of personal choice for the benefits of being together. For some reason the word "compromise" has assumed a pejorative sense. In fact it is the most primitive human art of all: the skill of sacrificing a lesser good to gain or preserve something better.

The thought that we can, in a substantial way, determine our future without reference to fixed external necessities or to other people is fantasy. Like any other daydream its principal effect is to diminish our capacity to interact with the real world. And mostly our imaginings about potential prospects do not pay enough attention to the reality of inherent sin which is well able to ruin the most elegant scenario with its sooty touch.

When Benedict talks about "desires" to be neutralized, we should understand these in the sense of anything that inclines us to act in a particular way. It is not only a question of things we want or strive after.

Our desires are often unconscious. They drive us in a particular direction without our being sure why we want to go there. Sometimes desires assume a disguise, and that becomes very confusing. We think we are pursuing one goal and all the while it may be evident to others that it is something else that we are seeking. This is especially so when there is a disproportion between the object of our interest and our zeal in cultivating it or our satisfaction in acquiring it. Sometimes we are not the best judges about the rationality of our behavior.

Desires incline us not only to seek what we think we want, but also to avoid what we dislike. Sometimes people are very controlled about giving themselves actively to the pursuit of something, but give the game away by their unreflective reactions and disproportionate antipathies. Again the real reason for rejecting or resisting something is not always clear to the person involved. He or she may be able to present an excellent case to justify certain conduct, but often it is just camouflage. "Methinks the lady doth protest too much."

Humility helps us to know the restraints under which we live even though we do not yet have the capability to be quit of them. Sometimes it is easy to look back over our past and to see in retrospect the measure of our unfreedom. Now that things have changed for the better we can look more squarely at the way they used to be. It is not too difficult to acknowledge past encumbrances. But, generally speaking, we are so desperately ashamed of our present liabilities that we don't even want to think about them. We do not want to acknowledge the concrete dimensions of our need for salvation. As a result we find self-knowledge a fearsome prospect.

It is true that many people do psychological tests. Seminars on personality types and the enneagram are always well-attended. The frequency of self-assessment quizzes in *The Reader's Digest* seems to indicate that people find such pursuits entertaining. Generally the context of these tests is to define an area in which action is possible with a view to self-improvement. In other words, it is not a question of coming to one's limits. No experience of desperation is involved; no plaintive cry for help. It is usually the workaday task of finding out what can be done and devising strategies to produce the desired results. All this is very good. But it is not the same species of self-knowledge that comes from discovering that one cannot save oneself.

The amazing thing is that our experiential knowledge of God begins with our discovery of our own finiteness. We can learn theology and psychology until we are blue in the face, but such knowledge will not bring us closer to God apart from the humiliating acceptance of our own limitation. This point was made eloquently by the fourteenth century English mystical writer who composed *The Cloud of Unknowing*.

> And therefore toil vigorously, as far as you can and will, to get for yourself a true knowing and feeling of self, wretch as you are. And then, I believe, soon after that you will have a true knowing and feeling of God as he is...as he allows himself to be known and experienced by a humble soul living in this mortal body.[1]

Our task, for the moment, is to uncover the
nakedness that we have been frantically trying to
conceal since we left Eden. Brazenly to accept the shame
because it is part of the truth. The other part of the
truth is that our feeling of shame in no way reflects any
attitude of God. Julian of Norwich says this beautifully.

> For we shall verily see in heaven without
> end that we have grievously sinned in this life,
> and not withstanding this we shall verily see that
> we were never hurt in his love, nor were we ever
> of less value in his sight.[2]

The untruth resulting from concealment is more
offensive to God than any apparent ugliness revealed
by honest admission. Trusting in love we take the risk
of facing up to reality. If our feelings of shame inhibit
our doing this, then we should pray for the boldness to
override them.

It is humiliating to acknowledge that we are enslaved by sub-personal forces. It is, however, the truth
of the human condition, as the seventh chapter of the
Epistle to the Romans attests. Sin is not an abstraction.
It takes a unique, concrete shape in every person, intri-
cately weaving its identity from the skeins of individual
experience. This is why no program of spiritual growth
can be detailed that is applicable for all seasons of
everyone's life. Sin is the ultimate individuator. The
battle against sin must, in consequence, be nuanced in
each case. This is why spiritual warfare has to begin
with an appreciation of the precise configuration sin
assumes in the life of a particular person. Likewise, the

action to be taken must be tailored to fit the unique situation of each.

At any one of the several beginnings that I experience in the spiritual life I need to take stock. I have to ask myself, "How does sin express itself at this point in my life?" We can examine ourselves with the help of Cassian's list of vices: gluttony, lust, avarice, anger, sadness (*deiectio*), purpose-lessness (*acedia*), vanity, pride. We can choose from later additions: sloth, envy, acquisitiveness, ambition, domination. We can ask ourselves whether we are enslaved by resentments or guilt based on past experience or by prejudice. Are we wracked by fears, uncertainties and self-doubt? Do we have a desperate need for love and affirmation that makes us drown our truth beneath an acceptable exterior? Is our imagination the playground of obsessions or compulsions? Do we find our lives blighted by substance-abuse, addiction or codependency? Have we lost substantial contact with objective truth, the demands of human solidarity or the consequence of our spiritual nature? If we plead innocent on all these counts we are probably deluded. If we discover that we are hopelessly mired in one or other of them, then we have cause to celebrate. The immediate steps to be taken, if we aspire to spiritual progress, are clear. We simply begin to struggle against whatever holds us down, trusting in the help of God. We don't hope for immediate victory. But, confident in divine grace, we try to water down our vices (RB 49.3). We probably will not be able to banish them completely—especially if they are linked with the fundamental fabric of our personality—but at least we can attempt to moderate their influence on our practical behavior (RB 49.4). In fact the whole program of monastic life—with its observances of vigils, fasting, work and chastity—is designed to keep in check these fundamental tendencies. Many of the difficulties in daily fidelity are not to be measured on the scale of obedience or conformity with external obligations. The real cause of these minor rebellions goes deeper. It is hard to maintain one's fervor in these observances because the specific effort required runs counter to basic forces within our nature and reveals to us the extent to which we have not yet submitted our whole being to grace.

~ 32 ~
*Rather he imitates by his deeds the Lord's saying:*
*"I have come not to do my own will,*
*but the will of him who sent me."*

In his staunching of the flow of desire the monk is not motivated principally by his zest for the attainment of a certain level of spiritual fitness. It is true that some of the ancient writers used to talk about monks as spiritual athletes, but I am uncomfortable with this description. It seems to me that striving for abstract perfection is a boring and narcissistic way of spending one's time on earth. This is why Benedict immediately introduces at this point the theme of the imitation of Christ.[3] Christian monasticism is not a Christian version of the universal phenomenon of monasticism. Rather it is the monastic way of being a Christian. Being a Christian is primary. Benedictine monasticism is not an end in itself; it is simply one way of following Christ. In RB 4, Benedict makes this point explicitly: "To deny

oneself to oneself in order to follow Christ." Self-denial
and self-control are only means to an end; what matters
is the following of Christ.[4]

Fervent discipleship is at the heart of Benedictine
spirituality. The monk is fired by a great love for Christ,
he is open to be guided by Christ and he is willing to
deny his own inclinations in order to put Christ's
teaching into practice. This is what is meant by describing
the Benedictine way as Christocentric. Whatever
asceticism or self-denial is involved in following this way
serves only as an instrument to safeguard the primacy
of the monk's Christian discipleship. He is, above all, a
man who is loyal to Christ. His commitment is
unconditional. He remains stable even when he
understands nothing. His will is firm even when times
are very hard.

This discipleship is closely linked with humility.
Both involve submission to Christ as master—not being
oneself the controller of one's life. The negative aspect
of this commitment is more visible to the observer: a
monk is one who gives up much by virtue of his state
of life. As a rule we are less aware of the more important
component of a monastic vocation that is beneath the
surface. What great love there must be to cause a man
to give so much, to endure so much and to demand so
little for himself![5] Self-control and self-denial are
significant because, when they are authentic, they
indicate that love is beginning to displace selfishness in
the details of daily life.

Our discipleship involves us in a lifetime situation
of being open to formation by Christ.[6] This involves
acceptance of his word in the myriad ways in which it

comes to us: through *lectio divina*, through conscience, by other human beings, in the events that Providence designs or allows. Our saying "yes" to Christ is conditional upon our willingness to say "no" to ourselves. If self-will is our first priority, we can never be followers of Christ.

~ *33* ~
*Scripture also says,*
*"Will deserves punishment; necessity wins a crown."*

The quotation is not from the Bible but from the literature of martyrdom.[7] By using it a little out of context the Master and Benedict both want to draw attention to the value of submitting to necessity. Experience leads us to the conclusion that following self-will is a sure means to disappointment in oneself, disapproval from others and ultimately condemnation by God. People who contrive always to get their own way are rarely happy, they are not liked and they do not grow. Desire is really a very tyrannical master, although while it governs our lives it will not allow us to perceive this negative impact. Any prolonged exercise of self-will injures our integrity, whether its purpose is the direct pursuit of pleasure or, more indirectly, the avoidance of pain. To the extent that our will is concerned principally with pleasing ourselves we can anticipate trouble. On the other hand, learning to live with situations that cannot be changed is a gauge of maturity and a valuable means of preserving our peace of soul.

The negative dynamic involved in doing God's will consists in breaking the nexus between desire and action. We cannot immediately eliminate desire—it is part of our concrete humanity. For example, we cannot expect to be able always to subject the promptings of lust or envy to reason, because part of the functioning of the passions is to edge out the cooler operations of the mind. Perhaps the first step is to learn to recognize the dimensions of our sub-personal propensities, to slow down a little, to weaken the link between desire and action. In this way we get into the habit of interposing some personal control on our behavior so that the external expression of desire or aversion ceases always to be immediate and automatic. We introduce a moratorium, a cooling-off period. In this way we are less overwhelmed by the urgency of present feelings and more likely to be able to weigh possibilities within the context of our personal choices regarding the direction of our life.

*~ 34 ~*
*The third step of humility is*
*that a monk for the love of God*
*submits to his superior in all obedience,*
*imitating the Lord of whom the Apostle says:*
*"He became obedient until death."*

The third step of humility is a concrete application of the second. It also involves the doing of God's will and the setting aside of one's own desires in imitation of Christ. The means to this end is now given as obedience to a superior.

St Benedict's doctrine of obedience is so important that we need to see it in the context of the whole Rule. In particular, we have to avoid the facile comparison of monastic obedience with that demanded in the army, business or other totalitarian organizations.

> Military obedience completely subordinates the individual to the totality so as to give more strength and coherence to that totality. Monastic obedience, on the other hand, does not pursue a social goal but one that is quite individual. It clearly is at the service of the ascetic perfection of the individual.[8]

From its beginnings in the desert monastic obedience derives an emphasis on its formative role. Obedience makes a man into a monk not because doing what one is told is *per se* monk-making, but because it is part of a relationship that allows a man to be formed into monkhood. If obedience worked automatically, then the army and the various bureaucracies would be full of monks and nuns! It is not the fact of obedience that monasticates but its content. Obedience is the means by which monasticity is transmitted from one already formed by years of monastic practice. This is why St Benedict emphasizes the teaching aspect of the abbot's position and those of his appointed officials. The abbot's task is not only to give orders but, by instruction and example, to create a climate of meaning in which monastic priorities are paramount. This demands of the monk not only a willingness to obey but an openness to having his perspectives changed.

Before it expresses itself in compliance with commands, obedience is an act of listening.[9]

To some extent the desert *abba* has been coeno-bitized in the process of being transformed into the Benedictine *abbas*. The change reflects the well-attested pattern seen when charismatic leadership is replaced by hierarchical or institutional authority. The abbot envisaged by St Benedict is the head of a smoothly-running organization. He may not have the personal flair for spiritual direction that was evidenced in the apothegmatists of the desert, but neither is he an autocrat. Unlike the contem-porary civil rulers, the abbot described in the Rule operates within constitutional limits. His task is not to impose his own will or to dominate others but to be a spokesman for Christ (RB 2.2), his authority curtailed by the Rule (RB 1.2, 3.11, 64.20) and by the injunction that he "is not to teach, establish as policy or to give orders outside the Lord's precept, *extra praeceptum Domini*" (RB 2.4). Note the use of *extra*. Not merely *contra*, which would have signified anything opposed to the Lord's word. The abbot is seen by Benedict as a mediator of Christ's message, not an originator of a teaching that is substantially his own. He is the steward and not the owner of the monastery (RB 64.7)— a perspective in RB that deviates from the Master's view of the abbatial prerogatives.

The authority that Benedict gives to the abbot is a power to facilitate growth in the monks. In fact, the word *auctoritas* derives from the verb *augere* and means fundamen-tally one who promotes the growth and prosperity of others. The determinant of genuinely authoritative action is not the needs or wishes of the one in authority, but the situation of those on whose behalf authority is exercised. Benedict was aware of this.

> [The abbot] must be aware that he has accepted a difficult and arduous task: that of ruling souls and being at the service of many different persons' way of living. One he has to cajole, another rebuke and a third persuade. He must conform and adapt himself to the condition and intelligence of each in such a way that he suffers no loss to the flock entrusted to him, but rejoices in the growth of a good flock. (RB 2.31-32)

In interaction between abbot and monk, it is the abbot who has to adapt himself not the monk. The abbot is at the service of different characters: *multorum servire moribus*. Nowhere is it said that a monk has to defer to the whims and caprices of the superior.

The Benedictine abbot is not the source of God's will but merely the mouthpiece. One of his principal tasks is to weigh up situations with a view to discerning which course of action may be more in conformity with Gospel priorities.[10] Far from it being his prerogative to have his preferences christened "God's will", the abbot is more obliged than anyone else in the monastery to leave aside his private partialities. It is his duty to seek out what may be the most divine among many options. Sometimes this demands much self-denial and a great deal of patient labour. Benedict recognizes that God often speaks through other people. Therefore the abbot must be a listener. God gives light through the community and often, as St Benedict notes, through the young (RB 3.3).[11] The abbot is expected to see in real events and situations a call for a modified response: the age and intelligence of the monks (RB 30.1, 38.1), the needs and infirmities of individuals (RB 34.1-2, 38.2, 53.19, 55.21-22, 66.5), the gifts of God (40.1-2, 57.1), the demands of extra work (41.4-5), the call of hospitality (42.10, 53.10), the climate (55.2). If a visiting monk makes a reasonable suggestion the abbot is prudently to examine the matter, "lest it happen that the Lord has brought him in this direction for this very purpose" (61.4). Benedict recognizes that groups of local Christian vigilantes or even bishops can be channels of divine guidance and intervention (64.4-5). It is important to realize that Benedict does not offer a positivistic view of authority: the abbot does not decide on his own lights what is the will of God. Rather, it is his duty first to seek it and, only when he has found it, to communicate it to his monks by teaching, policy decisions and particular commands or prohibitions. Benedict never prescribes as a condition for abbacy that the applicant should be a man of prayer. It must be obvious, however, that if an abbot is negligent of his own spiritual life he will not long continue operating within the very exigent parameters that Benedict has set for him.

The third step of humility can be better interpreted if we understand the counterpart of obedience in the Benedictine view of authority. If humility requires submission to authority, the quality of that action will be determined by the quality of the authority to which one submits oneself. To submit to wise and enlightened leadership is common sense and to rebel against it immaturity. Benedictine obedience cannot be assessed without appreciating just how much the Rule requires of those who exercise authority in the name of Christ.

The attitude of the one giving submission can be deepened by reading the fifth chapter of the Rule which deals with obedience. And we should not forget the qualifications added by Benedict at a later stage of the Rule's composition. One example is RB 68, about the resolution of difficulties that may arise in particular circumstances, and another is RB 71, in which Benedict sees such advantage in being cooperative and considerate of others' wishes that he wants the monk to be obedient to everyone—so long as good order is not disturbed.

Benedict is not much interested in compliance as an act of social harmony. He promotes obedience as a quality that heightens the evangelical character of life when accepted in a spirit of love. In the third degree of humility, St Benedict has added to the text of RM the qualification "for the love of God". Benedict is always far more concerned for the subjective dispositions with which an act is done than the external effects it produces.[12] The monk obeys on the understanding that his submission will help to increase his openness to God by receiving direction and by his imitation of Christ's salvific self-emptying.

This is the opposite of slavish compliance. It is a mature, calculated attitude. The motive power of obedience in the desire for eternal life (5.10). Benedict realizes that obedience is the narrower way, yet ultimately it leads to this goal (RB 5.11). On the understanding that monks are essentially seekers of eternal life, Benedict views obedience from this angle rather than as a means of social control. "They no longer live by their own judgement, yielding to their whims and appetites; rather they walk according to another's decisions and directions, desiring to live in monasteries and have an abbot over them" (5.12). This is why, mixing up his steps a little, Benedict declares, "The first step of humility is unhesitating obedience, which comes naturally to those who cherish Christ above all" (5.1).

Monastic obedience is a theological, Christological and eschatological reality. It is not the result of a timid personality nor is it the outcome of social manipulation from one side or the other. It is a freely-chosen way of life, vowed by the monk to God (RB 5.3, 58.17). Although it is not without "fear of the Lord (RB 5.3, 5.9), its primary energy comes from an act of personal adherence to the teaching and example of Christ. Because obedience is the path that leads to God (RB 71.2), it is animated by hope, by the fervent desire for eternal life (RB 4.46, 5.3) and by trust in the fidelity of God (58.21).

It is because of its spiritual character that monastic obedience has none of the sly fictiveness characteristic of institutions everywhere. This obedience, however, will be acceptable to God and agreeable to human beings only if what is ordered is done boldly, promptly, enthusiastically and without grumbling and overt reluctance (RB 5.14).

Benedict expects the monk to obey in the spirit of cheerfulness indicated by 2 Corinthians 9.7: "God loves the cheerful giver". Even though he may experience difficulties in this fundamental monastic observance, the monk needs to bear in mind that it is obedience, above all, that will help to bring him to his goal. An honest attempt to live in conformity with

God's will prepares the soul for contemplation, the experience of which blots out the memory of the blood, sweat and tears which preceded it. And after this hundredfold can be expected the even greater gift of eternal life.

When it comes to understanding obedience as constituting the third step of humility, we need to remember that it is obedience as seen in a benign light. Becoming a monk is not a vocation to be a doormat. Apart from those strange moments when it seems part of God's formative program for us, such degradation is normally not God's will. As such, deliberate humiliation is not to be seen as a means of coming closer to God or of increasing our capacity for salvation. More often it is, rather, a function of human sinfulness. Of course the system does not always work as smoothly as Benedict hoped. Coping with abuses of authority and the inevitable unfairnesses of community life will be discussed in the following chapter. It forms Benedict's next step.

## Notes

[1] Modernized from the Middle English text in Phyllis Hodgson, *The Cloud of Unknowing and the Book of Privy Counseling* published for the Early English Text Society by Oxford University Press, 1944. Chapter 14, p. 42.

[2] Edmund Colledge and James Walsh [ed.], *A Book of Showings to the Anchoress Julian of Norwich* (Toronto: Pontifical Institute of Mediaeval Studies, 1976), Chapter 61, Revelation 14; p. 603.

[3] For a general survey of this theme see E. J. Tinsley, *The Imitation of God in Christ: An essay on the biblical basis of Christian spirituality*

(London: SCM Press, 1960). Also the articles in the *Dictionnaire de Spiritualité*, 7, cols 1536-1601. This series of contributions does not include a treatment of the Hellenistic content of this theme in patristic authors. See also Giles Constable, *Three Studies in Medieval Religious and Social Thought* (Cambridge University Press, 1995), pp. 143-248: "The Ideal of the Imitation of Christ".

[4] Some modern authors distinguish between "following Christ" and "imitating Christ", giving historical precedence to the former. See Richard Yeo, *The Structure and Content of Monastic Profession: A juridical study, with particular regard to the practice of the English Benedictine Congregation since the French Revolution* (Studia Anselmniana 83; Rome: Edizioni Abbazia S. Paolo 1982), p. 97. A closer study of the philosophic background of the phrase in Christian literature makes this unlikely. See Simone Deléani, *Christum Sequi: Étude d'un thème dans l'oeuvre de saint Cyprien* (Paris: Études Augustiniennes, 1975), pp. 27-32. According to this author, Christian usage is distinguished from pagan, by its strong affective content, an element not unrelated to its association with martyrdom.

[5] In Adv 3.3 (SBOp 4.177) Bernard of Clairvaux argues from the very fact that monks give up so many precious benefits that their level of spiritual enlightenment is higher than they think. If they had not been somewhat conscious of an intimate spiritual attraction, what other reason would lead them to the monastery? In the modern world where there is a strong emphasis on conscious experience, we need to be reminded that sometimes experiences are so deep that they make little impact on consciousness and can be known only by their effects. In this case, actions surely speak louder than words or overt experiences.

[6] The collect for the seventh Sunday of the year in the current English version of the Roman Missal, expresses the content of this theme and its link with the mindfulness spoken about in the first step of humility. "Father, keep before us the wisdom and love you have revealed in your Son. Help us to be like him in word and deed."

[7] The original quote has been inserted in the *Passio Anastasiae* and concerns the disparity of fates awaiting those who sin for pleasure and those who are forced to perform sinful actions unwillingly. "Pleasure (*voluptas*) merits punishment; necessity wins a crown" (*Acta Sanctorum* [April], 1.250.) A similar sentiment is expressed by the fourth-century African bishop Optatus of Milevis: "Will (*voluntas*) has punishment; necessity, pardon" (*De Schismate Donatistarum* 7.7 [PL 11.1098b] or 7.1 [CSEL 26.160]). In the manuscripts of the Rule a certain interchangeability is observable between *voluptas* and *voluntas*. There is a related text in Augustine's tractate *On the Gospel of John* (26.4; CCL 36.261): "The poet can say (Vergil, *Eclogues* 2), "All are drawn by their own pleasure (*voluptas*)." It is not a case of necessity but pleasure. It is not obligation but delight." Another non-scriptural text cited as if it were from the Bible occurs in 7.61, a quotation from Sextus used twice by the Master (RM 9.31, 10.81).

[8] Translated from Pierre Miquel, *La vie monastique selon saint Benoît* (Paris: Beauchesne, 1979) p. 95. He bases this conclusion on K. Heussi, *Der Ursprung des Mönchtums* (Tübingen, 1936), p. 241.

[9] That is why, in many languages "obedience" and "listening" are similar words. For instance, in Latin, *obedire* and *obaudire*.

[10] See M. Casey, "Discerning the True Values of Monastic Life in a Time of Change," *Regulae Benedicti Studia* 3/4 (1974/75), pp. 80-81.

[11] See M. Casey, "Taking Counsel: Reflections on RB 3," *Tjurunga* 37 (1989), pp. 12-19.

[12] See Adalbert de Vogüé, *Community and Abbot in the Rule of St Benedict* (CSS 5/2; Kalamazoo: Cistercian Publications, 1988), pp. 432-434, "Care for the Inner Life". Perhaps the French *Souci de la subjectivité* would be better rendered, "concern for subjective dispositions". Vogüé writes, speaking of RB 68, "Nowhere does one better see what RB has added to RM: a more refined sensibility [sic] towards the inner life of the monk, and an educational effort more devoted to that life. . . A study of RB in its entirety would

disclose that such terminology recurs wherever the redactor has set
his seal on the Master's résumé. It witnesses at once to an interest in
the how of the observance and in the qualitative and interior aspect
of the actions performed by the monk, and also to an ardent zeal,
which seeks to communicate its own fervor."

# VII
# Patience

Those who enter monasteries and many others who seek to live a more intense spiritual life often climb the first degrees on the ladder very quickly. Bernard of Clairvaux is of the opinion that the first two steps have to be taken before entry into monastic life.[1] This is not to deny that they may have to re-climb these elementary steps later in their progress. The point is that most of the readers of this book will have arrived at this fourth step at least once. Despite the appearances of an unruly generation, many today are genuinely searching for guidance in life; they are generous in giving themselves and willing to be directed.

The first difficulty experienced by many is in the area of coping with what they perceive as an abuse of their trust. The way of obedience often demands that we go beyond the limits we have drawn for ourselves. This exposes us to the fear and uncertainty that characterize unfamiliar territory. Our hard-earned skills become irrelevant and we find ourselves in a situation for which we feel ill-prepared. We may consider ourselves (sometimes correctly) as victims of inefficiency, mismanagement, exploitation or unfairness. Anger and sadness may constantly dog our steps, fueled by a wounded pride and seething imagination. Suddenly all our efforts of the past seem to have been wasted. Due to the defects of others, we say, we find ourselves worse off than when we began. Spiritual lightness is lost and progress seems to stop. It is at this point that many feel that it is time either to abandon the spiritual quest or, at least, to redefine it to the point of practical extinction. There are people who terminate their monastic adventure simply because it asks of them the sort of sacrifices for which they once thought themselves ready.

This is the situation that, in Benedict's mind calls for patience. Not the trivial domestic virtue we sometimes associate with this term, but a global assent to having our lives imprinted with the character of the paschal mystery. "Who could have believed that crime consists less in making others die, than in not dying oneself?"[2] The great obstacle to growth in the spiritual life is seeing it exclusively in terms of activities, forgetting that it inevitably involves a degree of passivity; specifically it includes suffering. Without becoming maudlin or masochistic, each of us has to give assent to the measure of suffering that is part of our destiny.

St Benedict wants the newcomer warned of the hard and difficult things to be encountered on the way to God (RB 58.8), and this is a gesture that is both kind and prudent. No one escapes negativity, though its forms vary with individuals. We are not permitted to think that, if we had been treated well, we would not have had to endure hardship. Though suffering is a universal human phenomenon, its shape is largely determined by inner factors, conscious and unconscious. We are often wrong to attribute crucial significance to external events. The truth is that we carry within us toxins that have to be neutralized. The process of detoxification must go on if we are to make progress. God in his love for us will allow us no respite until the remedy has achieved its effect. Inevitably the process of reversal will draw its components from our situation, but it is our inner state and not the outward events and actors that make purification necessary. Sometimes it takes us many painful years to learn this.

St Benedict's teaching on patience, largely copied from the Rule of the Master, is one of the most important parts of the Rule. Because of potential misunderstanding of the nature of patience it is well worth pondering in a prayerful and reflective mood. To internalize this value is to give stability to our following of Christ and more realism in matching reality with lofty ideals.[3]

~ 35 ~
*The fourth step of humility*
*is that when this obedience*
*[involves] hard and contrary things,*
*or even when there may be undeserved injuries,*
*his mind quietly embraces patience.*

The first obvious point is that Benedict links patience with the demands of obedience. Having given such a priority to obedience, it is not surprising that St Benedict recognizes that it will be in this area that the monk will be most insistently tempted. Apart from whatever is necessary for the probation of novices (RB 58.3, 11), Benedict does not envisage the abbot deliberately making life miserable for anyone. But his long monastic experience convinced him that, even with the best will in the world, it is rare for an abbot not to make demands on his monks' patience. A sensible monk will take for granted that living at another's behest will be unpleasant at least some of the time. The Master is more sanguine in this matter and has no qualms about the severity of obedience, seeing it as the monk's mode of martyrdom.[4]

> For the Lord's sake their will is frustrated every day in the monastery and they patiently bear as a martyrdom whatever commands are given to test them. (RM 7.59)
>
> Finally, even in a time without persecution when Christianity is at peace, we do our military service in the school of the monastery under the abbot's command through trials and frustrations of the will, so that when, after the pilgrimage of life in this world, our Lord summons us to judgment, we may present to him our worthy deeds, offering him our patience with all the diverse and difficult things that the abbot commanded us and which we willingly undertook for God's name, as also the different frustrations of our wills which we gladly bore for God's name and the soul's salvation. (RM 90.29-32)

Both these texts continue with the quotation of Ps 44:22, also cited in the present context.

St Benedict has an extraordinary string of words to describe the negative aspects of life in a monastic community.

|                          | Verse # in RB 4 |
|--------------------------|-----------------|
| Hard things              | 35              |
| Unfavorable things       | 35, 38          |
| Undeserved injuries      | 35, 42          |
| Suffering                | 38              |
| Testing                  | 40              |
| Examination by fire      | 40              |
| Being led into a trap    | 40              |
| Tribulations             | 40              |
| People over one's head   | 41              |
| Adversity                | 42              |
| Being struck on the cheek| 42              |
| Having one's coat stolen | 42              |
| Forced to walk a mile    | 42              |
| False brethren           | 43              |
| Persecution              | 43              |
| Being cursed             | 43              |

Here, as elsewhere, Benedict is not afraid of a little hyperbole. While this list does not represent a completely factual description of every monastic life, it does make the point, with the aid of a few apposite scriptural images, that monastic life does have its hard times. As indeed does any human life, notably if it involves some form of community existence. Cannily, Benedict nowhere speaks of a monk reaping the harvest of his own errors. In recommending patience he speaks as though the monk were completely blameless in the unfortunate situations that occur. Most people feel that way even if, objectively speaking, there is no basis to the presumption of innocence. Benedict is clear that anyone who is earnest about following the monastic way will encounter many troubles; to survive monastic life patience is an absolute necessity.

Benedict places considerable emphasis on this virtue, seeing it as the means *par excellence* by which the monk enters into the experience of Christ and so is transformed. It is especially through his sharing in Christ's Cross that the monk dies to self and enters into the subjectivity of Christ. He begins to have the mind of Christ, sharing his awareness of the Father and being animated with his boundless compassion for the weakness and pain of fellow human beings.

> Never quitting [Christ's] *magisterium*, but persevering in his teaching and [living] in the monastery until death, we will by patience become participant in Christ's passion so that we may also be worthy to be consorts in his kingdom (Prol 50).[5]

Patience is not mindless endurance. It is an acceptance, in union with the sufferings of Christ, of whatever pain life brings. It is not the quantum of suffering borne that sanctifies, but the willingness to relive in one's own situation the form of life chosen by Jesus for himself. What matters most is our practical acceptance of the way of Christ.

Suffering is the real test of discipleship. Fair-weather followers are easy to find. It is only fidelity in hard times that proves the genuineness of love. This is why Benedict wants to know how novices handle difficulties and humiliations (RB 58.8). Bearing with misunderstanding and harshness not only witnesses to inner

steadfastness: often it has effect of concentrating effort .
and strengthening the soul. A young tree that is too
protected from the wind never develops a sturdy root
system, whereas the apparent callousness of leaving the
seedling somewhat exposed makes for stability and
growth in its maturity.

The means by which we gauge whether hardship
is likely to lead to patience is the monk's state of mind.
It is not so much the magnitude of events or the degree
of pain which is the measure of patience. True patience
is marked by tranquillity in all circumstances. Here we
have to avoid quantitative judgments. We know from
experience that it is sometimes harder to remain calm in
small matters. Major disasters bring to the surface our
best qualities. It is the itch of petty pricklings that
particularly provokes our rage. Many are the heroes of
major battles who fall by ambush in unguarded
moments. Patience is not to be deferred until a major
calamity strikes; it is a disposition worth cultivating in
all the minor reverses of daily interaction. One of the
great characteristics of a genuine monk is interior quiet.
An aggrieved mind will never attain contemplation.

The last phrase in verse 35 has been transmitted to
us in several different versions. Here we see the
development from Cassian's *Institutes* to the *Rule of the
Master* and thence to RB. We also see a variant reading
of the text, almost certainly not authentic, but found in
many ancient manuscripts and illustrating the manner
monks traditionally interpreted the verse.

Inst 4.39.2    *in omnibus servet oboedientiae ansuetudinem*
               *patientiaeque constantiam*
               in all things he keeps obedience's meekness
               and patience's constancy

RM 10.52       *in  ipsa oboedientia...tacite patientiae*
               *constantiam amplectatur*
               in this obedience quietly he embraces
               patience's constancy

RB 7.35        *in ipsa oboedientia...tacite conscientia*
               *patientiam amplectatur*
               in this obedience...quietly consciousness
               embraces patience

RB 7.35        *in ipsa oboedientia...tacita conscientia*
               *patientiam* [variant] *amplectatur*
               in this obedience...with a quiet consciousness,
               he embraces patience

The development of this text illustrates how Benedict was able to introduce a new idea into the context with only a minor change to the words. The shift from the tautological "patience's constancy"[6] to a simple "patience" and, perhaps, a change in the subject of the verb from an implicit "he" to "consciousness".[7] Benedict makes the mind or consciousness the key element in patience. It is less a matter of mere endurance (important though this be) than of deliberately quelling the surgings of an aroused indignation. As Abba Joseph says when speaking of preserving a friendship, "First the monk must maintain tranquillity not only in his lips but also in his breast, whatever the injuries of which he is the victim."[8]

Aelred of Rievaulx lists six stages to be passed through in the attainment of peace of heart and tranquillity of mind.

- The rejection of worldly standards, particularly the search for pleasure or possessions and the ambition for honors,
- The setting aside of self-love, vanity, pride and the comparison of self with others,
- Reflection on the necessities to which one is subject, as a creature subject to the desires of the flesh,
- The experience of one's one infirmity, i.e., one's incapacity to do good and resist evil,
- Learning to place a guard over one's mouth and to be disciplined and restrained in speech,
- The practice of bodily stillness and stability in all one's undertakings.[9]

## a) Unworldliness

A monk will never be content or happy so long as there is an inconsistency between the inclinations which practically govern his behavior and the austerity of monastic life. Until he attains a measure of purity of heart, there will be many elements in the concrete conditions of monastic living that will upset him. Much impatience stems from the imperfect internalization of basic values. One whose formation was superficial will never be at peace in a community in which monastic values are paramount. Which values? Obedience, humility, silence, austerity of life, communal discipline, separation from the world. In other words by those values which collectively form a kind of self-denial that is fixed by communal standards and not by personal preference. These components of the monastic lifestyle will continue to irk so long as the values they presuppose are defective in an individual. In this case the inner disturbance which we label impatience is not a pure reflection of the state of the community, but is mainly a function of interior disarray.

*b) Unselfishness*

A narcissistic regard for self and all its works makes life in a community miserable. In a community of twenty five we can realistically expect no more than 4% access to particular community resources if others are to enjoy an equitable share. To seize more than that is to impinge on the rights of others. Wanting to have the community revolve around our particular priorities of the moment is a never-ending story. All of us always want more attention, more understanding, more intervention on our behalf. As a result we can be resentful of time and energy devoted to others or any effort made to encourage us to put the community first. To claim much from others on our own behalf is a certain recipe for an unhappy life. If we want peace of mind we have to work to change this situation, to learn to be content with little. This theme will return when we come to discuss the sixth, seventh and eighth steps of humility.

*c)Honesty*

There is a constant temptation to see our troubles as the result of factors external to ourselves. It is true that persons and events sometimes work against us. Their capacity to hurt us, however, depends on our inner fragility. Often we may conclude that there is something inside us that silently conspires with external factors, a certain unconscious victimhood, for instance, that acts as tacit invitation to violence. This is not to deny the culpability of those responsible in certain situations, but it is to suggest that our complicity contributes something to the pain we feel. To know ourselves and our sensitivities can help us to be careful in situations where our response has dispropor-tionate power to disturb our peace.

*d) Experience*

We who want to be strong sometimes cannot bear the feeling of powerlessness. So we avoid situations that might reveal our weakness or, if that is impossible, we blame others for the outcome. To be unafraid of confronting our limitations and having them known to others is to exorcise many demons. This is especially true with regard to interior weaknesses. Those who are not strong physically are constantly reminded of the fact and their infirmity is patent to all. Those who lack mental acumen are usually ignorant of the fact, because to be stupid is precisely to be unaware of one's stupidity. Likewise, there are people of notoriously bad judgment who never doubt their power to assess situations and devise remedies. Some of the most trying human experiences come from being forced by events to confess one's own obtuseness in perception and imprudence in action. To hear it said of us that we meant well! For many people the cracking of the carapace of a false self-image is a painful but necessary prelude to a renewed spurt of personal and spiritual growth. Often the choice is not ours, we do not have to do anything. Human life sometimes demands of us nothing more than endurance. There are situations that cannot be avoided, but must be borne. If we have faith and our will is stable in its adherence to God, then although the source of pain may be incomprehensible, its grinding negativity can be sustained. Furthermore, within the experience of our own difficulties is often concealed the complementary sense of God's mercy. At the end of our tether we cannot deny our need for salvation and, by that very fact, we have entered a state in which it is possible for us to receive the gift of God.

### e) Restraint of Speech

Our tendency when upset is to talk, often in uncreative ways. Sometimes we use our tongue to transmit our own pain to another so that we cease to be alone in our suffering. Usually it is not the person who hurt us that is the object of our attack: often we strike out at one nearby who loves us. Alternatively we can talk about our troubles not to ease them but to reinforce them, and especially, to strengthen the link between particular incidents and our habitual interpretation of their meaning. The repetitious recital of a log of grievances does nothing to bring peace but usually disturbs both the speaker and the one who listens. In troubles it is good to keep one's mouth closed, beyond a single, disciplined account to someone able to restore us to peace.

## f) Stillness

The Desert Fathers had two practices which eased some of the emotional anguish of the monks: remaining in one's cell and manual work. We will find both therapies helpful. Just as mobility is often a symptom of interior troubles, so remaining still can ease the situation. A still body, remaining in a familiar environment coupled with the avoidance of acedia can often prevent the monk from denying his difficulties and force him to face the exigencies of the situation that has developed. On the other hand, disciplined manual work provides a useful break when self-scrutiny becomes too intense. The exertion involved in external labor dissipates the kind of depression that follows too much inactivity, and simultaneously enables some of the pent-up physical energies to be leached off.

The truly patient monk is one who has trained his mind to look beyond present pain to ultimate realities. Patience is, accordingly, a work of faith. Without such a vision suffering is meaningless. There is no doubt that negative experience is the great challenge to faith and a source of temptation to abandon one's commitment. It is also true that patience has a purifying effect on faith and commitment and leads to a more naked definition of selfhood. One who has survived suffering knows that personal integrity is independent of goods and status and owes nothing to the attitudes and actions of others. It is the quality of a heart that has been hammered into humanity by this most universal of human experiences.

Having established this principle, St Benedict now emphasizes the importance of endurance. Once suffering and hardship are accepted as philosophically inevitable, the measure of mental confusion they occasion is reduced. But there remains the need to grit one's teeth and survive the scourging that Providence sometimes arranges for us. To be reconciled to a life-threatening disease and the prospect of death is a great advance, but there still remains the daily pain resulting from the illness itself and from the attempts to provide a remedy. A "theological" patience does not exempt us from the agony and anguish that must necessarily be endured.

~ 36 ~
*[The monk] endures [hardship]*
*without growing weary or running away.*
*Scripture says:*
*"Those who perseveres to the end will be saved."*

~ 37 ~
*Again:*
*"Let your heart be strengthened; trust in the Lord."*

~ 38 ~
*Scripture demonstrates*
*that the faithful for the Lord's sake,*
*must bear everything, even contrary things.*

*It says in the person of victims:*
*"For your sake we are afflicted with death*
*all the day long;*
*we are reckoned as sheep for the slaughter. "*

There is a shift of emphasis in these verses, as though the focus has been lengthened. They begin with the need for endurance but this is quickly put into the context of an intense personal relationship with Christ. We see here how the spirituality of the ancient martyrs continues even without external persecution. In thinking retrospectively about one's own life one will often give thanks to God for difficult times, because it seems that it was at these times that one "discovered" Christ again. Brought low and at the end of one's own resources there was no other alternative but to invest in God whatever remained of hope. Perhaps the sentiment from Lamentations 3:26 will assume an importance at this time: "It is good that one wait quietly for the Lord's salvation." It is a time for endurance, waiting, quietness and, surprisingly, hope.

Nobody can know how difficult it is to remain steadfast under the particular trial which a person endures in solitary suffering. Every day we grow wearier, and the temptation is to abandon the spiritual pursuit even though it is inseparable from our spiritual selfhood. We may dream of escaping into mindlessness. We may seek activities to distract or entertain. Perhaps we teeter on the brink of mental betrayal—writing off the investment of many years as a bad debt and seeking to start afresh. At such times, life seems in ruins.[10]

It is at this point that Benedict brings out his heavy artillery. The feeling of failure or revulsion is so strong it may overwhelm us and it is only the contrary view of the inspired Scriptures that serves as a counterbalance to our sense of desperation. *Lectio divina* is especially needful at such a juncture. Benedict begins with the Lord's call to perseverance. There is a challenge here. Salvation is reserved to those who see their commitment through to its limits. Those for whom faith will provide comfort in the evening of life are those who have clung to it in labor and disgrace and have proved themselves to be more than fair-weather believers.

The connection between obedience, patience and perseverance is spelled out by a twelfth-century Cistercian Abbot, Isaac of Stella.

> Obedience welcomes the seed which is [God's] word; patience causes it to bear fruit but it is perseverance which harvests the fruit. As the Apostle said, using the image of athletes, "All run in the race, but only one wins the prize." So it is possible to say about the virtues: all of them run toward God's kingdom, but only one of them receives the prize. Contempt of this world runs, poverty runs, the keeping of vigils runs, almsgiving, abstinence, obedience and patience all run. Only perseverance receives the crown. For it is "the one who perseveres to the end who will be saved", for the Lord judges the ends of the earth. The middle phase is no worthier of consideration than the beginning. It is not reckoned virtue to begin something, but only

to bring it to completeness. So, just as patience enhances obedience, perseverance crowns patience and makes it blessed. Patience exercises and tests obedience, perseverance brings patience to glory. May the Father through the Son in the Spirit deign to grant perseverance to us whom he has endowed with obedience and not left entirely bereft of patience.[11]

What powers patience is a progressive switch in the focus of consciousness. The patient monk tends to become less concerned with the humiliations and afflictions visited upon him and more possessed by hope in God. By dint of endurance the level of mental upheaval is reduced and the sharp pain of repeated attacks becomes a dull ache that blots out the awareness of distinct afflictions. Negativity is generalized and one's response is less to particular troubles and more like a fundamental stance. Instead of diagnosing each element and seeking to neutralize it, the monk begins to give his assent to the Cross of Christ and in its embrace discovers a love which makes hard times tolerable. Almost like a knight-errant enduring the rigors of wandering and war but sustained by his love of the lady whose champion he is.

In a mysterious way the experience of the deprivation of all temporal comfort—even consolation in prayer—leads to an intensified awareness of being bonded to Christ. It is this solidarity in being emptied, this shared diminishment, that often heralds a new depth of contemplative prayer. *Nudus nudum Christum sequi*: naked to follow the naked Christ.[12] The willingness to embrace the way of non-acquisition, non-achievement and non-recognition is also witnessed in the early Cistercian motto: *cum paupere Christo pauperes*: poor with the poor Christ.[13] It is not the diminishment that is primary but the sense of interpersonal communion with Christ. The quiet mind of patience results from the action of grace at a deep level that eludes our immediate awareness. Ascending the ladder of lowliness creates in us the dispositions necessary to welcome the gift of salvation. We cannot predict when God will intervene to give us a breathing space. Our task is to wait in hope. There is no other way to union with God. "Let your heart be strengthened; trust in the Lord."

The sufferings that come unbidden to one who has embarked on the spiritual ascent cannot be understood. There is a saving grace in this unknowing. Before God can impart his transcendent grace he must break in us our reliance on the linkage of cause and effect, and our confidence in being able to comprehend what is happening. The gifts of grace surpass human discernment. As long as we are bound to our own powers of assessment, no room is left for the God of surprises. We have to let go of our desire for mental control and let God act. When we resist this step, events will conspire to lead us into a profitable unknowing by the way of suffering for which we can perceive no cause within ourselves.

If there is no overt cause the probability is that our pain has a providential purpose.[14] We endure for the Lord's sake, exactly as the martyrs did. It may seem as though every day is an encounter with death, but we must learn to pray with that ancient hero of patience:

"Even if he kill me, still will I trust him" (Job 13.15).[15]
Our pain is meant to propel us toward God, not merely
to nurture our sense of grievance or to make us
withdraw more into ourselves. As God complained of
Israel: "They do not cry to me from their hearts, but
they wail upon their beds" (Hos 7:14). Suffering
becomes patience only when it is carried beyond itself,
when the wall of self-absorption is breached and we are
opened more fully to the healing touch of God.

*~ 39 ~*
*But secure in the hope of God's reward,*
*they continue joyfully:*
*"But in all these things we have overcome*
*because of him who loved us."*

*~ 40 ~*
*Elsewhere Scripture says:*
*"God, you have tested us,*
*you have tried us as silver is assayed by fire.*
*You led us into a trap,*
*and heaped troubles on our backs."*

*~ 41 ~*
*Then, to show that we ought to be under a superior, it*
*adds:*
*"You have put human beings over our heads."*

The motivation behind Christian endurance is
hope in God's gift of eternal life. "The sufferings of this
present age are as nothing compared with the glory that
is to be revealed to us" (Rom 8.18). This involves the

acceptance of the reality of a future life. "If for this life only we have hope in Christ then of all human beings we are the ones to be pitied most" (1 Cor 15.19). St Benedict does not attach to his chapter on humility the graphic evocation of heaven that the Master uses as conclusion. Benedict may have been a little dour or lacking in imagination, but there is no doubt that he repeatedly sets before his monks the prospect of heaven. In later centuries devotion to heaven will become one of the distinguishing marks of Benedictine monasticism.[16] Without such an eschatological perspective patience is impossible and monastic life will never attain its specific character.

One of the qualities we find emphasized in the ancient accounts of the martyrs was their joy. There is no question of finding pleasure in pain. Rather it is the joy that comes when everything is lost but love perdures. We always suspect that love attaches itself to our good qualities and we fear that it will be lost if they decline. In the days of our abundance we can never experience the unconditional quality of divine love. We secretly believe that something good in us attracts the love of God. It is often hard to go on believing when we discover how unlovable we are. But how great is the joy that follows the discovery that God's love precedes and prescinds from any human worth.[17] We are not defeated; Christ's love for us ensures the ultimate victory.

St Benedict then quotes from Psalm 65 to describe the range of trials we may expect, fiery temptation, a sense of being trapped (See Jer 20:7), and oppressed by many troubles—among which Benedict puckishly includes superiors. The interesting thing about this particular psalm is that it begins *Jubilate Deo omnis terra*: "Sing a joyful song to God all the earth." The verses quoted are not uttered in the depths of desperation, but they belong to the moment in which deliverance is proclaimed. Just as returned travellers often like to highlight the hazards of their foreign adventures as a celebration of life, so the Psalm lists all manner of human woes as yielding to the saving intervention of God. "Come and hear, all you who fear God, and I will tell what God has done for my soul" (Ps 65:16). Looking back on life we will be able to say that the hard times have also been times of grace, that God can indeed write straight on crooked lines.

~ 42 ~
*These are they who fulfill the Lord's command*
*by patience in adversity and injury.*
*"When struck on one cheek, they offer the other;*
*they release their cloak to someone who steals their tunic;*
*when forced to go one mile, they go two."*

~ 43 ~
*With the Apostle Paul,*
*they bear with false brothers and persecution,*
*and they bless those who curse them.*

In case it is not clear that the patience about which Benedict speaks is not a specific monastic trait, but is common to all Christians, this step of humility ends by evoking the Sermon on the Mount and the example of St Paul. Patience is the sum of Christian praxis. The kingdom of God is such a rich gift that it superabundantly compensates for the loss of goods or the need to endure the effects of evil.

## Notes

[1] Hum 49; SBOp 3.53.11-12.

[2] Albert Camus, *The Fall* (Harmondsworth: Penguin Books, 1963), p. 83.

[3] See M. Casey, "The Virtue of Patience in Western Monastic Tradition," *CSQ* 16.1 (1986), pp. 3-23. Reprinted in *The Undivided Heart*, pp. 95-120.

[4] On this theme, see Edward J. Malone, *The Monk and the Martyr*, (Washington: Catholic University of America, 1950).

[5] This is a very labored and literal translation of a verse that is not easily rendered into English. It is one which Benedict has added to the text of the Master and, so, is all the more precious. Unusual for Benedict is the alliteration resulting from the profusion of p's.

[6] This construction is probably what is called an epexegetical genitive, whereby two words that are closely related in sense are joined into a single emphatic expression. On this little-appreciated yet much-used literary device see Basilius Steidle "Der Genitivus epexegeticus in der Regel des hl. Benedikt," *Studia Monastica*, 2.1 (1960) pp. 193-203.

[7] This is the sense adopted in *RB 1980*. Others such as Lentini and Vogüé understand it as meaning "he quietly embraces patience with his mind", reading *conscientia* as an ablative rather than nominative. The sense is similar in both interpretations.

[8] John Cassian, *Conference* 16.26; SChr 54.244.

[9] Aelred of Rievaulx, *Sermones Inediti* (ed. C. H. Talbot, Series Scriptorum SOC, 1; Rome: Editiones Cistercienses, 1952), "Sermo Beate Virginis," pp. 141-142 with a recapitulation on p. 144.

[10] See M. Casey, "The Deconstruction of Prayer," *Tjurunga* 51 (1996), pp. 91-102.

[11] Isaac of Stella, *Sermon* 18.16-17; SChr 207, pp.20-22.

[12] On the background of this traditional axiom see *Dictionnaire de Spiritualité* 11, col. 509-513.

[13] *Exordium Parvum* 15.9.

[14] Sometimes there are causes which are not apparent in discussion. On the one hand, one seeking counsel may deliberately withhold data concerning certain behavioral aberrations. These are deemed irrelevant either because they are long-standing or because they seem unrelated to present difficulties. On the other hand, certain traumatic events of childhood may have been repressed, but unknown to the victims, continue to induce a heaviness and mistrust that seems to have no visible cause. Both situations render it difficult for the person undergoing trial to attain a point of clear-mindedness and serenity.

[15] During such stages in spiritual growth suitable *lectio divina* is a vital means of reaching the reframing that is necessary to make the transition to the next phase. Often the Psalms (especially the laments), Job, Jeremiah and the Book of Lamentations can be helpful. These can help to ventilate our rage and grief within the context of a deep but puzzled faith in a personal God.

[16] See Jean Leclercq, *The Love of Learning and the Desire for God: A Study of Monastic Culture* (London: SPCK, 2nd Edition 1978), pp.

65-86. Gregory the Great certainly contributed to this tendency. See J. B. McClain, *The Doctrine of Heaven in the Writings of St Gregory the Great* (Washington:Catholic University of America Press, 1956).

[17] This is the note on which Francis Thompson concludes his poem *The Hound of Heaven*.

> Strange, piteous, futile thing!
> Wherefore should any set thee love apart?
> Seeing none but I makes much of naught" (He said),
> "And human love needs human meriting:
> How hast thou merited —
> Of all man's clotted clay the dingiest clot?
> Alack, thou knowest not
> How little worthy of any love thou art!
> Whom wilt thou find to love ignoble thee,
> Save Me, save only Me?
> All which I took from thee I did but take,
> Not for thy harms,
> But just that thou might'st seek it in My arms.
> All which thy child's mistake
> fancies as lost, I have stored for thee at home:
> Rise, clasp My hand and come.

# VIII
# RADICAL SELF-HONESTY

The title of this chapter is taken from an article which well describes the background of St Benedict's fifth step in the ascent of humility.[1] The manifestation of secret thoughts to an elder was a central practice among the early monks, less for the content of the elder's response than for the self-knowledge it evoked in the monk.[2] Nor was it merely a matter of the presentation of sins for absolution, but the revealing of whatever filled the heart. Speaking honestly about oneself to an elder was considered a means of testing objectively the reality of private imaginations. If humility is truth then a significant part of its practice must involve bringing out into the daylight of another's judgment whatever is hidden and, therefore, subject to delusion.

It is the monk who is the primary beneficiary of such disclosure. It is not merely a means of collecting information helpful for the abbot's pastoral care in governing the community.[3] Taking the difficult step of speaking frankly about oneself is the price one pays for spiritual progress beyond a certain point. Encouragingly, it is also the sign that one has already made considerable advance in opening oneself to the workings of grace.

*~ 44 ~*
*The fifth step of humility is*
*that a monk does not conceal from his abbot*
*any evil thoughts entering his heart,*
*or any evils secretly committed by him.*
*Instead he confesses them humbly.*

The genesis of this verse, almost identical in both RM and RB, can be found in two of the "indications" of humility given by John Cassian:

> Secondly, if he does not conceal from his senior not only his own actions but also his thoughts. Thirdly, if he allows nothing to his own power of discernment, but entrusts everything to the judgment [of the senior] thirsting for his advice and gladly listening to it. (*Institutes* 4.39.2)

The three authors seem to emphasize "non-concealment" and there is a certain sense in which a relationship is defined by what is concealed. The real issue, however, is positive self-revelation. The abbot is to be regarded more as a physician than a policeman and hence he ought to be appraised of anything that secretly interferes with one's well-being. It is a principle that makes a lot of sense and is easy to enunciate. Nevertheless, its implemen-tation proves difficult for many people. If one begins to speak about this step of humility in a monastic community, one will quickly sense a certain uneasiness among the audience. There are several possible explanations for this.

## 1. Lack of Vocabulary

Some are so extraverted and estranged from their inner processes that they are unable to come to grips with the inner face of outward acts. Their normal volubility is reduced to silence when it comes to verbalizing what is invisible. Sometimes such people have to learn a new language before they can begin to talk about what is close to their hearts.

## 2. Mistrust

Some experience difficulty in trusting another with their secrets. Experience of the abuse of trust has engendered a certain wariness. In particular, many find it hard to approach persons in authority. Often those with serious problems tend to seek help from a marginal person in the community or an outsider, especially in cases where the official community is perceived as part of the predicament.

## 3. Fear of Intimacy

What is kept secret is intimate and to share that secret presupposes either anonymity or intimacy with the other person. Past confessional practice guaranteed the former. Shielded from direct contact and shrouded in absolute confidentiality it was possible to speak freely even with a total stranger. Intimacy, on the other hand, requires more investment. Beyond a naive confidence which usually leads to eventual disillusionment, the only trust that is worthwhile is one that has been patiently developed and tested over a long period of interaction. Inevitably that process sometimes suffers shipwreck halfway through.

*4. Shame*

Many of us do not want to be exposed. Shame is not the same as guilt, nor does it only concern things of which we are "ashamed". It is more like a fear about the future than a negative feeling about past actions. Shame relates to privacy—to those aspects of our existence that have not yet been validated by the affirmation of another. We are often fearful that another's acceptance is conditional upon our being "acceptable" in certain areas. We are reluctant to disappoint them by uncovering ugliness that we know others hate. We fear to risk rejection, so we gloss over the existence of a problem in the interests of preserving the relationship. The result is a barrier; the more we hold back, the less favorable the climate to broach the subject.

*5. Self-Sufficiency*

Occasionally one encounters people who believe that they are better qualified than others to judge their own situation. For them no purpose is served in revealing their secrets. Eventually it may happen that things become so unbearable that their reserve is broken and they do seek another's support. In other cases this willful solitariness leads either to much loneliness or to the complete abandonment of the spiritual pursuit.

*6. Avoidance of Challenge*

Some hold back from self-revelation because they do not want to be challenged. They are not interested in having another query their interpretation of events or advise on future actions. Sometimes these people avoid situations where serious discussion might develop, or they keep the conversation bubbling with endless inanities or they exclude feedback by controlling the agenda by presenting "problems" and "crises" that are not the real issues. Such stratagems of avoidance are often unconscious, but they prevent any healthy dialogue developing.

Because of these difficulties it is important that we pause at this step and attempt to appreciate what St Benedict is saying. He believes that after a monk has invested considerable energy in active good works and in the endurance of suffering, the time will come when he needs to avow that underneath the virtuous facade there remains much that is unredeemed. Despite his own efforts, he finds that his hold on monastic goodness is still very tenuous. For the future the way ahead consists in affirming one's need for salvation in concrete terms. This means confessing one's sinfulness to another person. In some paradoxical way, St Benedict believes, the very act of pleading guilty without any request for mitigation is a positive step towards healing and restoration.

Furthermore we need to remember that superiors are prohibited by canon law from doing anything that might be construed as forcing a "manifestation of conscience". Often they may have a shrewd idea of what is troubling us, but they are not supposed to help us by asking leading questions. The initiative is left to us. Most will not probe beyond the limits we indicate. I must make the decision to reveal myself, nobody else can do much to make it easier for me.

There are three further things to be noted about this verse. Firstly, St Benedict limits the content of the exchange to sinful thoughts and evil deeds; he speaks of "confessing" rather than of "confiding". This is far narrower than was the earlier practice. Secondly, although Cassian uses the word senior to describe the confidant, both RM and RB restrict this function to the abbot. This is to be expected from the Master, but one would have thought that Benedict would have coenobitised the practice, especially in view of the role assigned elsewhere to wise "spiritual seniors" (RB 27.2, 46.5-6). Thirdly, no mention is made of any response from the abbot. Perhaps we might reflect on each of these points.

### a) Revelation of Sins

Monastic life is a sustained program of good works. This is clear to any outsider who scans the daily schedule. It is true that there have been mischievous monks from the very beginning, but most find it less hassle to comply with the rules, roles and expectations of the community. The result is a life that is externally ordered and devout. It is usually unwise, however, to assess the quality of a monk's commitment on the sole basis of regular observance. St Benedict is very clear on this, both when he speaks of the criteria for professing novices (RB 58.8) and when he distinguishes "good zeal" from the "zeal of bitterness" (RB 72.1). Subjective dispositions are paramount.

The purpose of the relentless sameness of the monastic round is to create a climate in which hidden aspects of the personality become manifest. External monotony is an invitation to inner change whereas novelty and constant variety short-circuit the process of going deeper. Once the strangeness of the monastic existence has worn off and a certain level of evenness is attained, particular elements of one's inner life begin to make their presence known. Meanwhile there is no external change that others can know about. The monk becomes aware of thoughts and feelings that are at variance with his stated aspirations and external conduct and he is aware that sometimes these find expression in secret activities. When this becomes more than a transitory phenomenon he is forced to adopt a stance. He may compartmentalize his life so that the private sphere is split off from his public persona. He is leading a double life. Alternatively, he may rationalize his aberrations. This will cause his mind to be possessed by a basic untruthfulness. Thirdly, he may feel so badly about this inconsistency and his incapacity to improve matters that his commitment to the continuance of the monastic project is undermined.

Monastic life is not straightforward. It has its devious elements. These are appreciated by the survivors, and it is their experience that can help those at an earlier stage. Only a very small portion of this existential truth, however, can be communicated through formal teaching or by books. We all believe that we are different, and we follow our feelings to the conclusion that somehow the normal teaching does not apply to us. No matter how much instruction we are given on the pitfalls of spiritual progress we will still be unprepared when the moment arrives. Almost the only way the tricky turns of monastic life can be negotiated is by the personalized, interactive communication of traditional wisdom at the right time. This means that when life gets into a mess the most likely way out will be by telling someone the raw details of our situation and allowing ourselves to be guided by their response.

It is our contrary thoughts and our failures that we are most likely to conceal. Or more accurately it is those aspects of them which are the most intimate that we are reluctant to broach. There are people who develop a skill of rattling on about certain sins, all the while avoiding anything which might reflect badly on them. If we are to reap benefit from this practice, we have to be prepared to go beyond comfortable limits, to act contrary to our sense of shame, to ignore our own blushes. The support and encouragement another can give us will be in proportion to the ruthless honesty of our self-disclosure.

One immediate effect of talking about our secrets is that they are thereby more firmly fixed in our consciousness. Just as a dream is quickly forgotten if we do not reflect on it, write it down or discuss it, so many intimate spiritual experiences gain more cogency by being spoken about. In the interchange the basic components may be reframed in the light of the other's response—more centrality being given to one element, another allowed to centrifuge. Our assignment of priorities becomes more realistic and objective in the process. By revealing our resolutions to another we are supported in our efforts to upgrade our life. The important thing to remember is that all these good effects will follow only if the unveiling of self is integral. If we consistently exclude the negative aspects of our experience, our self-portrait will be inaccurate and the other's response will be proportionately off the mark.

I spoke about "integral" self-disclosure. We will never go much closer to totality than this. Our picture of ourselves is more like a line drawing or even a cartoon than a photograph. A desirable quality in one to whom we reveal ourselves is the capacity to fill in the gaps intuitively. Good guides draw on wide experience to hear what we are saying even when the words we use are inadequate. Although some people find it easier to start the process by dropping their particular bombshell, it often seems more natural to move gradually from the general to the specific as the relationship develops. In this way a context is built up in which the meaning of particular aberrations can be more accurately gauged. Also, there is a greater level of mutual trust to cushion the impact. Here we have to remember that moving away from our natural impulse to conceal our faults is not the first step of the ladder. St Benedict seems to imply it is a stage which takes place only after a certain consolidation of monastic values. Before this, it may be inferred, we are more inclined either to be protective of our secrets or to be selective in our revelation of them. We fear to be known as we are.

If another person can look squarely at my sinfulness I will be empowered thereby to accept this aspect of my reality without cringing. I will say to myself, "So this is the way sin is expressing itself in my life." That we are sinners should occasion no surprise. What does come as news is the manner in which sin is concretely embodied. Another's acceptance may ease the way for me to see myself as I am without losing my nerve. With the help of God I may then allow myself to become dissatisfied with this state of affairs and soon be ready to let grace propel me in a different direction. In this movement lies growth and happiness. Concealment leads only to stagnation and gloom.

### b) Abbot or Another?

This insoluble question highlights a dilemma that is typical of monastic history. How far can the spiritual and free-wheeling aspects of the monastic charism be reconciled with its institutional and hierarchical form? In the desert there was no problem. The monk spontaneously approached the elder of his choice. In a Benedictine community one abbot is elected—usually for an extended term. The reasons for his election are manifold; a mixture of inspiration, the candidate's personal qualities, political realities and current community needs. Election is no guarantee that an abbot will have the capacity to make people comfortable in revealing their negative qualities, to understand what they mean and to respond creatively. The issue is whether an abbot and a monk should continue if a process is not working.

Should they attempt to define the terms of interaction more realistically and/or should the monk, with the abbot's blessing and encouragement, seek someone else in whom to confide?

This is a topic that is too delicate to answer in universal terms. It concerns not only the abbot but other officials who are appointed to an office which includes—for want of a better term—an element of spiritual direction. On the one hand there is the danger of a monk not being helped because of his sense of alienation from official channels of help, on the other, there is the danger of subversion and political division within the community (RB 69.1-3). As a minimum basis of a solution I would suggest that each monk should try to have as broad and deep relationship with his abbot as reality allows, and he should be open to improving that bond. The abbot, for his part, should ensure that the functions he cannot personally perform are fulfilled by others in his name and in the name of the community. It is not subversion but subsidiarity. This already happens in the case of deans (RB 21), the prior (RB 65), the formator (RB 58.6) and in the looser category of "seniors" mentioned above. In the case of evil thoughts rising from the unconscious, Benedict twice suggests that they be immediately smashed on the rock that is Christ and once adds that they be later revealed to a spiritual senior (RB Prol 28, 4.50) In this latter text the abbot is not specifically nominated. Probably it is good that there are several in a community to whom access is encouraged in difficulties. Church law guarantees this in regard to sacramental confession. It will usually happen spontaneously where monks need to speak to someone about themselves. The difference between communities is that in some the possibility of wider consultation is regarded as normal, in others it is viewed as subversive of the abbot's authority.

There is a danger, however, in "shopping around". Being too free with one's secrets relativizes the seriousness of the self-disclosure. One's sharing of secrets can degenerate into a mere recital of a familiar tale with the object of comparing one hearer's response with another's. Having sought a second (or twenty-second) opinion one is entitled to choose between the options. The momentousness of sharing the horror of one's personal sin is lost and the power of the other's reaction is proportionately diminished. The element of risk is halved with each new confidant and the possibility of a long-term relationship decreases. Those whom we, in the course of a lifetime, trust with our most intimate secrets should be no more than can be counted on one hand. Beyond that there is a real possibility that our sense of selfhood will be violated.

To confide in someone is to have faith in them as a source of human solidarity or as a channel of divine guidance. It may happen that these complementary functions do not coincide. In times of total puzzlement about our immediate actions, we will often find it useful to follow the example of the Magi and consult King Herod. When our difficulty springs from a chronic sense of being alone and lost then it is more likely that we will turn to the angel Raphael for a cure of our blindness and bitterness. It is unrealistic to expect to find all qualities in a single abbot. His role as a revealer of God's will is part of his office and is aided by a grace of state. A capacity to offer fraternal support to a monk in difficulties more often depends not on the abbot's aptitudes but on the monk's personal past. Despite good intentions on both sides, an abbot may sometimes come to the conclusion this more horizontal kind of assistance needs to come from another source.

The good thing about choosing to confide in one's abbot is that there is an inbuilt stability about the relationship. A choice of a personal confidant can be easily reversed. In such a case one may regret one's former frankness and, additionally, one will face the prospect of beginning afresh with someone else. Sometimes such a relationship may be terminated unilaterally as a means of evading a challenge. Everything goes well while we speak and the other listens. Then the point arrives where the other intervenes, perhaps to pose a question or to draw our attention to some inconsistency or blind spot. Our response is to feel hurt, betrayed, rebellious. If we break away at this point we may simply be running away and leaving a basic issue unresolved. It is harder to escape from an abbot, whose pastoral care for us goes beyond the limits of personal interaction. In any case we need to make sure that we do not quickly lose trust in one whom we have chosen as a confidant—especially when that person wishes to address some matter that we would rather leave undisturbed. We have to continue believing in the soundness of our first judgment that the other was trustworthy.

## c) The Other's Response

It could be said that the most valuable element in Benedict's practice of confessing one's sins to the abbot is speaking one's secrets in the hearing of another human being. The focus is on the speaker. Once spoken the word can never be retracted; it exists as an object in the awareness of the other person. It is the radical honesty to self that is liberating and therapeutic rather than any response that the hearer might make. Sometimes it is the tranquillity and acceptance of the other's listening that is more important  than any words or suggestions which might follow. But it is the cathartic act of speaking one's shame and owning one's personal sin that clears the way for progress.

In recent decades attention has been given to the value of the non-directive interview. In such a context, the prime activity for the counselor is listening. This is not the same as being withdrawn, distracted or so empty-headed that one has nothing to say. It is a respectful and receptive silence which invites the other to speak and signals accurately that the communication has been received. It involves postponing judgment indefinitely. Much discipline is required in offering to persons in distress a secure situation in which there will be no recrimination but an active effort to appreciate their side of the story. There is no compulsion to offer immediate remedies to solve the problem but only a willingness to sit quietly with another's pain.

Some measure of this quality is demanded of abbots or of any who attract the confidences of others. The act of hearing what another says is already a response to their words. From the monk's point of view the most agreeable surprise comes when he realizes that even the dark portrait of himself which he has agonized to present does not rupture the other's respect, acceptance and love. What he craves is some sign that he has been fully understood and that the relationship is unchanged. Usually this asks more than a professional equanimity. Some personal gesture is called for, the code for which depends on the reality of the relationship.

Sometimes a more explicit reply is desirable. Its cogency will depend on whether this more fundamental response has been communicated. There are four ways in which a good word may be spoken in such a situation. Perhaps it is better not to speak about asking and giving advice. It seems likely that a more nuanced vocabulary would be clearer.

As a fellow-Christian the abbot may speak words of counsel. Both abbot and monk share the same Spirit and have access to the gift of counsel. Entering into sphere of communion in the Holy Spirit together they may perceive reality in a new light. When two gather in the name of Christ sometimes God's will imposes itself in their minds, without either having to work consciously to produce a solution.

As an elder with many years' seniority in monastic life the abbot may be able to relocate the monk's experience within a broader context, drawing from his own hard-earned wisdom and his familiarity with tradition. This is especially important when a monk is going through one of the phases of decon-struction, when his whole life slips into disarray and there seems to be no viable monastic future. Only experience can convincingly advocate a course of action that runs clear contrary to immediate impressions.

As a tested friend the abbot can offer a monk consolation in times of hardship, as well as support and encouragement in opting for what is best. By solidarity, empathy and prayer he can powerfully aid a monk in his task of turning away from evil and doing good.

As superior of the community the abbot can help the monk by occasional correction. For every ten acts of praise, affirmation and approval, he will have one chance of offering a correction. Sometimes this will be for the individual monk's own good, at other times it will concern his standing in the group, the welfare of others or the peace of the community. Nearly always such feedback will cause a degree of strain at least temporarily, but if the relationship survives it will become stronger because of the intervention.

There is much to be hoped for in an intimate relationship with one's abbot. If it is infeasible in practice, it may be that some of its functions can be filled by others. There is no need to stand alone. It is foolish to condemn oneself to an unprofitable solitude merely because one is reluctant to admit in oneself the sins which are the common lot of humanity. St Benedict's advocacy of openness is clearly a doorway through which we can advance to greater obedience to grace. It is a hard step, but one that yields great benefits.

But it takes two to tango! The abbot must have the human qualities, the willingness and the time to enter into the mystery of another's subjectivity. For the moment he needs to set aside other preoccupations in order to be present to the being of the monk, to his history of salvation and his sin. The monk, for his part, needs to overcome his embarrassment, his complexes about authority and whatever might tempt him to hold back. For both it needs to be an adventure in theological faith and an exercise in mutual trust. Both need to be aware of the danger of playing unconscious games, especially using the opportunity as a means of manipulation. The success of the enterprise depends on both.

St Benedict leaves us in no doubt of the value he places on such an intimate relationship between the abbot and the monk. It is a difficult ideal to realize. It is, however, worth pondering. Perhaps there is more to what Benedict says than meets the eye at a first reading of the Rule.

~ 45 ~

*Scripture admonishes us about this:*
*"Reveal your way to the Lord and hope in him."*

*~ 46 ~*
*Again:*
*"Confess to the Lord, for he is good;*
*his mercy is for ever."*

*~ 47 ~*
*And again the Prophet:*
*"I have acknowledged my sin to you;*
*my unrighteous deeds I have not concealed."*

*~ 48 ~*
*I said: "Against myself will I denounce*
*my unrighteous deeds to the Lord,*
*and you have forgiven the wickedness of my heart."*

Again we are faced with a barrage of scriptural admonitions. The interesting point is that they all concern confession to God rather than to another human being. It seems that Benedict in some way equates confession to the abbot with confession to Christ, even though primitive abbots were not priests and there is no question here of the sacrament, strictly speaking.

One of the perennial characteristics of the Catholic tradition is its insistence of human mediation in the work of salvation. The abbot is understood primarily as one with the quasi-sacramental role of doing the work of Christ in the monastery: teaching, healing, calling, leading. St Benedict saw him as an icon of Christ. An abbot's major struggle is to live up to this lofty ideal. A monk who approaches his abbot *qua* abbot is not merely having recourse to a brother's expertise. He is approaching Christ through faith in the person of one called to act in his name. He has the right to expect from his abbot a response equally based on faith. He has a right to seek the mercy of Christ in the face of his abbot. It has often seemed to me in that those monks who are blessed with an abbot who embodies the attitudes of Christ have less difficulty in maintaining their hope in God's mercy (RB 4.74) than those whose abbots are severe, distant or preoccupied. I often hear monks exhorted to base their dealings with their abbots on faith. Maybe abbots should also be admonished to ensure that their contacts with the monks habitually go further and deeper than ordinary human interchange.

So, one who takes his Christian life serious and enters a monastery has to learn self-control, obedience and patience. After that he needs to move towards a greater level of honesty with himself through being open with another. This leads to a radical sense of validation in which the monk develops such confidence in his spiritual identity that he is prepared to let go of many lesser goods. In particular he no longer has to cling to a false facade, he is prepared to be and to be seen as subordinate. And this leads to the next three steps of Benedict's ladder.

## Notes

[1] Columba Stewart, "The Desert Fathers on Radical Self-Honesty," *Vox Benedictina*, 8.1 (1991), pp. 7-53.

[2] There was a story of a monk who fruitlessly fasted for seventy years in order to understand a passage in the Bible. Seeing that his labor was vain, he set off to ask his brother. An angel met him on the way and revealed the meaning, saying, "these seventy years you have fasted have not brought you nearer to God, but when you humiliated yourself by going to see your brother, I was sent to tell you the meaning of the saying" (See Benedicta Ward [trans.] *The Wisdom of the Desert Fathers* (Oxford: SLG Press, 1977), p. 50.) The point is that it was not his brother's answer that brought enlightenment, but his own humility in setting aside his efforts and subjecting himself to another.

[3] Although it is hard to see how a monastery can be well-governed unless its pastor understands the personal situation of each monk. On the empowering effect of telling one's story see M. Casey, *Towards God: The Western Tradition of Contemplation*, (Melbourne: Collins Dove, 1989), Chapter 12, pp. 134-147. Revised Edition (1995), pp. 133-146.

# IX
# ABASEMENT

The next three steps of humility concern the lowering of self-esteem and the acceptance of a inferior or non-controlling status in the community. From the point of view of the individual these are difficult steps to understand. From a more social angle they are a little more acceptable.[1] Nobody contributes less to the common life than those who constantly make demands or attribute absolute importance to their individual desires over the needs of the community as a whole. It may be inferred, therefore, that the monk who makes few demands and is happy to give way to others will be regarded as a considerable asset in any community.

There is a problem here. St Benedict recognizes in his chapter on good zeal that subjective dispositions matter. So, when he recommends abasement, he must be regarded as doing so with qualifications. Abasement is a useful means for curbing our wayward or excessive tendencies to domination, acquisition and social approval. Some people, however, are not ruled by such tendencies. In them there is an unhealthy need for the denial of self, which finds expression in some of the practices covered by the sixth, seventh and eighth steps of humility. They have a need to be subordinate and to submit passively to the wishes or whims of others. They easily admit error, accept criticism and confess their own mistakes. They are suspicious of praise, success or good fortune. They are naturally yielding. In their case some of the recommendations that are helpful for others become destructive.[2]

From this we may deduce a special need for discernment regarding abasement. There is a bias in religious life which rewards those who are comfortable in subordinate positions, who are open to guidance and correction and who conform to the standards and expectations of the group. Passivity and compliance are tacitly inculcated while the original, the outspoken and those with initiative are subject to an inordinate level of official criticism and bureaucratic blocking. The result is to advance as the model of a "good monk" one who is loyal to the status quo and submissive to the powers that be. In some people such abasement represents heroic sacrifice; in others it is merely a necessary outcome of their own psychological needs. For them it makes for a compatible and unchallenging life, but they often stagnate, especially if superiors are happy to play the game with them.[3] Not everyone needs to practise the same virtues. This is why Gregory the Great insists that the pastor know the character of those in his charge in order to prescribe what is appropriate for each.[4]

We have to exercise a certain amount of care in the interpretation of these three steps of humility. In the first place we need to recognize that their practice presupposes considerable monastic experience. It is not to be recommended indiscriminately to newcomers. Secondly, abasement often needs no more than a little encouragement; it comes almost naturally to one who has a certain level of spiritual experience. Thirdly, those who feel immediately drawn to practise abasement should probably forget about it. Their attraction may well be no more than the expression of a neurosis. On the other hand, one would certainly recommend continuing reflection on the topic to all those who feel repelled by what St Benedict wrote. His words may serve as a good counterbalance to their innate enthusiasm for self-exaltation.

*~ 49 ~*
*The sixth step of humility is*
*that a monk is content with all that is little esteemed*
*and with the least of everything*
*and judges himself a bad and worthless worker*
*in everything he is given to do.*

*~ 50 ~*
*He says to himself with the Prophet:*
*"I am brought to nothing.*
*I am ignorant.*
*I am no better than a beast before you,*
*yet I am always with you."*

The most important element of the sixth step of humility is not the lowly status of the monk but his contentment. The real monk is a man whose happiness is not dictated by changes in outward prosperity. "Where your treasure is, there will your heart also be" (Mt 6:21). Everyone passes through times of adversity: the sign of one whose heart is becoming uniquely fixed on God is that these external fluctuations have less power to affect moods. Patience has helped to cultivate a quiet mind and self-disclosure has made one less inclined to subterfuge. What remains to be done is to deny to external realities any automatic domination over our state of mind. This is a tranquillity which is not rapidly gained

The foundation of a renunciation of status-conferring goods and positions-is the personal realization of the dignity that is common to all Christians. My identity and status are not dependent on the good will of the abbot. They derive from being created unique by God my Father, redeemed by Jesus Christ my brother and uniquely gifted by the Holy Spirit. I belong to the communion of saints, all of whom recognize me as one of themselves. I don't need a stripe on the sleeve to convince me that I have worth. The approval and affirmation of others and the oppor-tunities these present are important to me, but if I lose them I am not automatically bereft of standing in the eyes of God. The contrary may be true since Jesus said, "That which is highly esteemed by human beings is an abomination before God" (Lk 16:15).

The word "content" is very dear. It bespeaks a happy state of mind that is deeper than sensual gratification or mere high spirits. It is as though the heart were able to leapfrog present reverses and find its joy in what is invisible and intangible. I ask for nothing more. "Having food and something to cover ourselves we are content" (1 Tim 6:8).[5] "Give me neither poverty nor riches, give me only the food I need to eat" (Prov 30:8). If I am satisfied with a little, then I will want nothing. It is not the fulfillment of all instinctual desires that makes for a blessed life but gradual reduction of the urgency of desire itself, and its subordination to our seeking of God.

A monk's contentment should be such that it is not fractured if his life is marked by *vilitas*. This noun from the adjective *vilis* is associated with being cheap, low-priced, valueless, paltry, common, mean, base. In concrete usage it sometimes approximates the notion of "having the status of a slave".[6] What St Benedict seems to be saying is that monastic life does not promise us that we will always have an upper-class existence: a good standard of living, esteem, leisure, culture and access to the fine things of life. While most monasteries can afford one or two gentlemen, it is more usual to anticipate a span that is ordinary, obscure and laborious. Some will inevitably receive more than others (RB 34.1-4). None may act as though the goods of the monastery belong to them (RB 32.4-5) and they will be called to account if they break anything (RB 46.2). The monks' clothing will be economical and unfashionable (RB 55.7). Sometimes the monks will be asked to do work that is both demanding and demeaning (RB 48.7-8). The monks are not to use their "monastic status" as a means of advancing their social level (See RB 53.6). A monastery is not a country club. Those who live there are expected to have opted out of the possibility of a career and a position in society. Whether slave or free, all alike can expect that sometimes they will be treated as a chattel, to be moved, used or left aside without any consultation.

The trick is to accept such treatment without losing one's self-esteem or becoming upset. "If we would welcome good things from the hand of God, why should we not also welcome the bad" (Job 2:9)? Patience has taught us not to look too closely at the immediate agents of our downfall, but to try to see all things with the global vision of God. When we pass through periods in which we bear the brunt of unfair usage we need, more than ever, to maintain the integrity of our confidence in God and in God's immutable plan for us. Although in human eyes the causal connection of the present with a desired future seems broken, things may be other than they seem. We cannot foresee the future and so we need to limit our downheartedness when things go wrong; maybe God plans the emergence of something better.

Nor do we have to be totally passive in such negative circumstances. Sometimes a setback is an invitation to redefine our goals, to find a way around an obstacle or, at least, to initiate some damage-control. We are not called to practise a tired and resentful resignation. Such an attitude would empty St Benedict's word *contentus* of all meaning. We do not deny present misery nor waste time in the baleful diagnosis of its causes. We accept what comes from the hand of God and use our own educated sensibility to guide us towards the outcome God intends.

So the monk may sometimes have to be content with the status of a slave and find himself the last in line for everything. It is no real consolation to say that this is probably a temporary situation. At the same time it is important to realize that part of the making of a monk is for him to pass through a stage in which alienation, failure and unpopularity are strongly experienced. When this happens he needs to get to the point where he looks to God alone for his vindication. All he can do is "eat and drink and enjoy his work as a gift from God" (Qoh 3:13). For the rest he demands nothing.

Others may intimate to him that he is a worthless and unprofitable servant. There are always a few members of the community who are ready with negative feedback. This reinforces the monk's inward sense of inferiority and increases his alienation.[7] So much "good advice" comes at exactly the wrong moment! If the monk can just interpose a distance between himself and his natural defensiveness, he may eventually come to the point of accepting that there is a certain reasonableness in others' negative assessment of him. This is a painful admission—especially after a prolonged bout of exculpation. But it is the way out of the morass. To see how much one has contributed to the sum total of misery in the world robs one of any right to plead innocent. In an act that is simultaneously self-knowledge and an experience of God, the monk buckles. He confesses that any good he sees in himself comes from God and any evil from himself (RB 4.42-43). He is happy to accept the Gospel description of himself as an "unprofitable servant" (See Lk 17:10).[8] It is not a rhetorical outburst declaimed in a state of depression, but an affirmation made judiciously and reasonably. As he advances in the spiritual life the monk begins to believe that he is a bad bargain.

It is a great grace when, in a moment of illumination, a monk sees that in some mysterious way what he suffers is the direct result of his own sin. It is not a question of punishment, but the direct experience of some of the previously hidden malignity of unrelieved selfishness. So much negativity is unique; others live in similar conditions without the pain I have. This is because my suffering is not only a function of external constraints; it is also the result of forces which I myself have unleashed. I will be needlessly unhappy until I have identified and accepted my own unwitting complicity in what has befallen me. If I do reach the point of peacefully accepting that I have received no more than I deserve, then my present pain will begin to act as a purge. Some of the accumulated plaque of selfishness will be chipped away. Life will become lighter.

Meanwhile a broad back is required. One has to consent to be treated as a plodding peasant or a beast of burden. This represents a kind of liberation both from the pleasure principle and from our compulsive rationalism. One learns to survive without success. One learns to endure without understanding. The senses are numbed and the mind is evacuated. From one point of view we have ceased to be human. But the humble monk is more than a mindless drudge. Beneath sense and thought a different zone of human reality is being activated. The heart or spirit is being set free. If such abasement is genuine then it leads rapidly to contemplation. The usual sensual and mental barriers no longer exist. Progressively the monk who seeks nothing else but God receives what he seeks. Firstly he gets nothing else. Secondly he gets God.

~ 51 ~

*The seventh step of humility is*
*that a monk not only proclaims with his tongue*
*but believes with the deepest feeling of his heart*
*that he is inferior to all and more worthless.*

*~ 52 ~*
*He humbles himself and says with the Prophet:*
*"I am a worm, not a human being,*
*one scorned and despised by people."*

*~ 53 ~*
*"I was exalted, then I was humbled and confused."*

*~ 54 ~*
*And again:*
*"It is good for me that you have humbled me*
*so that I may learn your commandments."*

There is a certain etiquette in monastic circles according to which it is considered bad form to blow one's own trumpet. The braggart will be quickly cold-shouldered in most monasteries. As a result conversation about self is usually characterized by understatement. Minimalism, however, can become a game. With a bit of practice in handling the code, it becomes possible to use self-deprecating discourse as a means of self-glorification, hiding one's liabilities and hinting at more qualities than one actually possesses. The decencies are intact but their purpose has been thwarted.

The use of such polite forms may be harmless: it merely adds a vaguely unworldly sheen to a monastic community in the eyes of those more accustomed to uninhibited self-promotion. There is another issue and this concerns the truth of such verbal humility and the genuineness of the relationships based on such a mode of communication. Is it right for a monk to continue using external forms which are at odds with his inner state? There is probably no harm in conforming to accepted etiquette so long as the monk does not think that humility is only a matter of external practices. To present by word and attitude a humble, docile and obedient front may be no more than pantomime. Benedict is not concerned with pious facades. It is the heart that must be changed.

A genuine attraction to be filled with the lowliness of Christ leads us to take steps to ensure that the press releases we issue about ourselves are truthful not only in fact but in implication. This means that they are made in the mindfulness of our own limitations and of the ugly scar tissue that remains. If we must boast of ourselves, let us boast of our infirmities (see 2 Cor 11:30). Practically, however, we cannot totally escape the necessity of speaking about ourselves. If we develop our willingness to speak from the heart, then the plain, unvarnished truth of what we say will be a help to others, whether it seems flattering to ourselves or not. In so much of what concerns humility we will find that the way ahead is indicated by forgetfulness of self and concern for others. Humility's opposite is always preoccupation with self. In this case the content of our conversation needs to be more for the other's advantage than for our own satisfaction.

What Benedict intends by this step is to draw our attention to the importance of inner conviction. Humble attitudes must derive from a deep experience of our own indigence. It is this realization that grounds our capacity to welcome the salvation Christ offers us. Such interior humility is not only a vertical attitude; if it is real it must extend horizontally as well. It is sometimes said at funerals that the deceased was humble before God, even while presenting a fearsome front to human beings. I wonder if this is possible. To be humble before God is to acknowledge that all is gift except what I have spoiled. I have more evidence of crime against myself than I have for any other human being. My conscience accuses me directly of so much malice, whereas I know only by hearsay of the evil done by others. To be humble before God is to know that I am blameworthy. If this does not influence my relations with others, then something is wrong. The experience of God is a revelation of my unworthiness. In this context, to believe that I am inferior to others and less meritorious is a realistic proposition.

This is not the same as a low self-image. It is a deliberate and sustained effort to be rid of the persistent delusion that I am guiltless. Empowered by the intensity of God's unconditional love for me, I find it possible to demolish my defenses and to admit the truth of my condition. There is nothing in my constitution or personal history that would give me any confidence in my own competence to bring my life to a happy conclusion. My trust must be in the action of God. My neediness is the counterpart of the divine abundance.

The psalms offer us many opportunities to give expression to such sentiments. It is possible that the Master and Benedict intend no more in this step than that we mean what we say when we sing the psalms. Benedict gives three examples. The first speaks of feelings of desolation when we are despised, scorned and rejected. The *opprobrium* mentioned here reminds us that one of St Benedict's tests for a good novice concerns his ability to deal creatively with *opprobria*. The second text deals with the up-down alternation, as common in spirituality as it is in human affairs.[9] The final text seems to be one that follows experience. It is retrospective. The times of trial are judged to have been profitable. They were good for me. The agent of the humiliation was not others not events, not even myself. It was the work of God. And the purpose of the process was continued schooling in God's law; to help me to learn the ways of God. It is impossible to conceive of anyone being wise without their having been through hard times. It is the discovery of God's surprising closeness when everything goes wrong that leads to a genuine spiritual wisdom.

The more we advance in monastic life and virtue the more aware we become of our own shortcomings and of our radical unfitness to receive the gifts of God. There are two possible responses to this insight. The first is denial: we work harder at self-improvement and self-fixing and simultaneously formulate a strong case to demonstrate that our situation is the fault of others. This leads nowhere. The alternative is to disenfranchise ourselves as the primary target of our philanthropy and begin systematically to put others first. This means deliberately choosing to assign a lower priority to our own needs and becoming somewhat altruistic. If we choose this option we are imitating Christ who did not please himself (Rom 15:3) but came to serve (Mk 10:45).

To be a servant is a very demeaning option. It is not enough simply to do servile tasks while secretly thinking of ourselves as destined for better things.[10] It is a matter of believing with the deepest feeling of our hearts that we are inferior to all and of less value. This should issue in a respect and admiration for others that makes us happy to put our time, energy and resources at their disposal. We become—in full freedom—their servants. It is not masochism or manipulation that makes us willing to serve, but the imitation of Christ, a love which desires our neighbor's welfare and a growing appreciation of the rightness of humility.[11]

~ 55 ~

*The eighth step of humility is*
*that a monk does nothing except what is recommended*
*by the common rule of the monastery*
*and the example of the elders.*

This short verse has caused a lot of anguish and annoyance over the centuries. It seems like the apotheosis of the status quo and the sounding of the death knell for any type of initiative.[12] It certainly makes for a very orderly monastery, especially if it is joined in facile combination with RB 63 (Community Rank) and RB 71 (That Brothers Obey One Another). In that conception, the monastery would be the ideal reflection of an Augustinian universe, with everything arranged in levels descending from God through innumerable mediating agencies so that each had a position and a code of conduct corresponding to it.

Of course it is a ridiculous model for a monastery. There is no place for meaningless hierarchies in a Benedictine community. There is one God, one Lord, one abbot. Every monk has direct access to all three. There is no need for intermediaries. For some unknown reason monastic institutions often end up trying to

mimic the very worst qualities of the world from which
monks have fled. There is no reason for a monastery to
follow slavishly the example of bureaucracies, factories
or bankrupt educational systems. Here is a prime
chance for interpersonal transparency, why replace it
with an impersonal array of committees, notices,
submissions and inter-office memoranda? Whatever
Benedict intended by this eighth step of humility, we
can be reasonably sure that he did not envisage
dehumanizing monasticism to the extent that the status
quo had the only claim to moral rectitude, and the only
way to operate was to go through the correct channels
and procedures.

The best means of building a healthy monastic
community is to choose to remain on the human scale.
This means a limitation in size and complexity. It
involves going without some technological possibilities
in order to pursue a simpler lifestyle. Most importantly
it calls for the development of mutuality in the
community—brothers being present to one another, not
lost in vast buildings, not hiding behind bureaucratic
barriers, not ensconced in one's personal array of
gadgetry. In practical terms communion is often the
result of the humdrum realities of coexistence,
cooperation and collaboration.

For this communion to have a lasting basis, some
contact is necessary at the level of monasticity. A monk
living in community cannot fashion a monastic ideal in
isolation. There must be an openness to receive from
others, particularly those who have advanced some
distance along the way. Most newcomers to monastic
life are prone to snap judgments about the quality of

life they see in certain members of the community. If they themselves survive, more often than not they will find it necessary to revise these self-indulgent assessments. As wisdom and humility grow, these monks will probably appreciate more the unique value of the lives of the seniors and find themselves looking to their example for encouragement and guidance.

We live in a universe that is different from Benedict's. Nowhere today do younger people look up to their elders as knowing more about the world than they do themselves.[13] Age no longer suggests competence. Seniority is not *per se* worthy of esteem. Whether we like it or not most of those born in the latter half of the twentieth century are loath to accept an extended period of apprenticeship as a method of acquiring knowledge or skills. Subordination to another person or to a system suggests a commitment and a level of trust in others that is rare. The result is that those entering monasteries, after an initial phase of compliance, begin to assert their right to act as they see fit. They do not see why they should model their behavior on that of others or be influenced by community precedent. Are they not more intelligent, better-formed, more conscientious and therefore better qualified to judge matters, than the unthinking herd of older monks?

There is not much point in trying to modify such an attitude too soon. Change will come with experience. Monastic life is rough enough to shake out some of this youthful priggishness. In fact it is often personal insecurity which makes people intolerant. Those who are genuinely at ease with their own level of attainment will have no hesitation about recognizing God's paradoxical gifts in others and being willing to earn from them.

From a junior's standpoint this eighth step of humility points to a future in which the need for "self-expression" and the pursuit of novelties will become less. The sooner this comes about, the fuller the realization of the monastic search for God and the happier life in the monastery will be. Reverence for the seniors is, perhaps, one of those areas of monastic practice where conversion is needed.

This step also challenges the seniors. If their example is to be the guide of community life, then it is incumbent upon these paragons to ensure their standards are high. Remember the old saying: "You catch more flies with a spoonful of honey than with a bucketful of vinegar." To influence others it is necessary to show that the living of monastic life is attractive. Not only that, but it is a worthwhile channel of guidance. Margaret Mead speaks about bridging the generation gap by presenting the past as "instrumental" rather than "coercive".[14] This means manifesting the capacity of tradition to enhance life instead of using it as a bludgeon to forestall discussion. The present situation has many unprecedented elements; these need fresh solutions. Existing answers often do not fit the questions.

There is, however, another element. The text includes the idea of the "common rule of the monastery". It is not unrelieved geriarchy. The Rule of Benedict insists that the community be governed with justice, fairness, moderation, balance, reasonableness, fraternity. It is not meant to be oppressive. There is scope for the juniors to be heard in community consultations (RB 3.3) and the possibility of appeal in difficult situations (RB 68.1-3). In addition, the constitutions of many Benedictine and Cistercian congregations promote such realities as active participation, co-responsibility, subsidiarity, initiative, communication and the welcoming of suggestions and desires. In other words, the legislation affecting the concrete governance of communities acknowledges the need for a more open community structure. This is for modern monks the "common rule of the monastery". Far from being excluded from participation, we are constantly urged to involve ourselves as fully as possible in all the concerns the polity of the community.

I once heard an interview with Herbert von Karajan, then the formidable conductor of the Berlin Philharmonic Orchestra. On being asked if he were an elitist, he replied, "No, I am a super-elitist." He explained further that he would not admit into his orchestra any who did not fulfill two essential conditions. "They must have the music within them, and they must play in time with others." Monastic life is the same. We must be in contact with our own unique sources of inspiration, but simultaneously we need to trim the expression of our own gifts so that there is no discord with others. It is harmony that is the ideal of a Benedictine community, not conformity or uniformity. In some ways the monastic choir is a clear symbol of the quality of community life. When differences combine to produce a rich and beautiful sound it would seem that you have a good community. On the other hand, a choir that is tense and ragged despite the presence of talented singers, probably indicates something amiss in the quality of community relationships. Concord is more a matter of persons being of one heart than of the soulless uniformity that comes from the imposition of a rigid code of standard behavior.

Perhaps St Benedict points to a balanced solution of the problems posed by seniority when he recommends that all "respect the seniors and love the juniors" (RB 4.70-71; 63.10). The challenge for the seniors is that their lives merit the reverence and honor that is given them. Juniors, for their part, need to be vigilant about their lovableness. Perhaps the greatest charity we can show our brothers is to make it easier for them to love us, and this sometimes provides the opportunity for more unselfishness than we might expect.

Meanwhile each of us is obliged to lubricate community life by any means at our disposal. Whether it is by blending with the group or by being somewhat distinctive, our motive needs to be the common welfare. One occasionally meets persons who are so fearful of being seen as conformists that they find it hard to submit to community standards and expectations in any way. They feel somehow obliged to be different. It is this neurosis that is being addressed by these three degrees, not its opposite.

The same vice of "singularity" which Benedict seeks to eliminate from the community is well chronicled by Bernard of Clairvaux in his treatise *On the Steps of Humility and Pride*:

> The common rule of the monastery and the example of the elders are insufficient for him. He strives not to be better but to seem better. His efforts are directed not at living better but as being seen to be successful, so that he can say "I am not like the rest of men". He feels better for one day's fasting while the others are eating, than

for seven days' fasting with everyone else. One little private prayer is more gratifying for him than a whole night's psalmody. At meals he casts his eyes often round the tables; he is pained if someone is eating less than he and feels defeated and begins immediately to deprive himself cruelly of what he had previously regarded as a necessary allowance of food. He is more afraid of loss of glory than hunger pangs. He holds himself as worthless if he perceives anyone thinner or more pallid than himself. He never rests. He cannot see his own face and hence cannot know how he looks to others. So he examines his hands and arms which he can see. He feels his ribs and runs his hands over his shoulders and loins to determine from the other parts of his body if he is too thin or not thin enough. Thus he tries to deduce the pallor or color of his mouth. He works vigorously at his own projects but is sluggish in community exercises. He stays awake in bed and sleeps in choir. At vigils, while the others are singing psalms, all night he nods off to sleep. Then after vigils, while the brothers are sitting quietly in the cloister he remains alone in the oratory. He clears his throat and coughs, and from his corner he fills the ears of those sitting outside with groans and sighs.[15]

As Bernard says elsewhere, "Do we laugh or cry over such foolishness?"[16] The problem is more than one of stupidity. In so setting himself apart from others, the self-absorbed monk isolates himself from the formative benefits that authentic community life brings.

Part of the truth of humility is living according to our social nature. For the monk in community, this means allowing himself to be formed by those among whom he lives. A harmonious community has a positive effect on the inner state of each of its members. It is not, however, an ideal that is easily realized even though major abuses are not present. In practice the greatest retardation is caused by harmful conversation: dissipation of energies, complaining, gossip and back-biting. So impossible is it to tame the tongue that Benedict prescribes a large measure of discipline and silence as means of ensuring that irrecoverable damage is not done. This leads us to the consideration of restraint of speech.

## Notes

[1] One who seeks to dominate others and control the life of the group is really denying the very heart of community life. A refusal to accept the diminishment of self-importance implicit in dialogue, negotiation, compromise and submission to the common will is tantamount to the denial of the reality of other members of the community. It is a very arrogant stance and one that isolates and eventually embitters. Manipulation is not always visible but it is almost always harmful both to the community and to individuals.

[2] To be distinguished from those who have strong abasement needs are those who seek to dominate or manipulate others by parading their own weaknesses and misfortunes. A group walking together goes at the speed of the slowest. The easiest way to exercise control over the group is not by aggressive self-advancement but by dragging one's feet and appealing to the compassion and solidarity of the rest. There are people who unconsciously use actual or exaggerated

difficulties as a means of circumventing a challenge or getting their own way. If I keep reminding the abbot about my susceptibility to migraine he may be reluctant to give me an assignment I don't want.

[3] In the area of power-abuse collusion is necessary. Just as an aggressor is impotent without a victim, so one who unconsciously seeks self-diminishment needs the collaboration of another who will move in to occupy the areas thus abandoned. Such mutual exploitation is occasionally seen in the sphere of spiritual direction when the client's need to be helped dovetails with the director's need to be a helper. The result is often comfortable for both but not usually creative on a long-term basis.

[4] In his *Pastoral Rule* Gregory devotes a chapter each to 34 pairs of character traits with indications on how to deal with the needs of each type. For example: How to admonish the insolent and the fainthearted (8), How to admonish the taciturn and the talkative (14), How to admonish the meek and the choleric (16). His point is that we need to recommend contrary virtues to those whose character is different. The text is found in *PL 77*. An English translation by Henry Davis is found under the title, *Pastoral Care* (Ancient Christian Writers #11; London: Longmans, 1950).

[5] This verse is quoted often in tradition as a witness to the appropriate monastic frugality, for instance in Cassian's *Institutes*, 1.2.1 (SChr 109, p. 38); 7.11 (p. 306), 7.29 ( p. 330). Bernard of Clairvaux also avails of the verse a dozen times. In *Apologia* 23 (SBOp 3.100 19-21) he adds the ironic comment: "As for us we are content only if we have all the food we can take and clothing that is becoming."

[6] There is a good note in *RB 1980* on this.

[7] Since I have used this word "alienation" several times, perhaps it may be useful to describe what I mean. I mean more than a chronic sense of bitterness or disgruntlement. Using Melvin Seeman's article "On the Meaning of Alienation" (*American Sociological Review* 24 [1959], pp. 783-791), we might conclude that a monk is alienated

when his values, actions and expectations lose their cohesiveness. This can be seen:

1. When the monk loses confidence that any change in behavior can improve his situation.
2. When his monastic life seems meaningless and he cannot predict where his own life is leading.
3. When he believes that the only way to achieve his personal goals is to ignore the "official" monastic norms and expectations.
4. When he thinks that being a "good monk" leads only to isolation and low approval in the community and so cannot see much point in it.
5. When he is estranged from himself and his values to the extent that monastic life has lost its intrinsic value and is assessed only on the basis of its perquisites.

[8] Nivard Kinsella OCSO wrote a book on humility under the title *Unprofitable Servants* (Dublin: Clonmore and Reynolds, 1960).

[9] Bernard of Clairvaux places considerable emphasis on this theme. See M. Casey, *Athirst for God: Spiritual Desire in Bernard of Clairvaux's Sermons on the Song of Songs*, (CSS 77; Kalamazoo: Cistercian Publications, 1988), pp. 251-280.

[10] This dissociative type of double existence is what Jean-Paul Sartre would term "bad faith". (See *Being and Nothingness: An Essay on Phenomenological Ontology* [Trans. Hazel E. Barnes] (London: Methuen, 1957), pp. 47-70.) It is very close to the heart of essential sinfulness. It twists our perception of reality so that, as a consequence, our responses to what we perceive are always off target. Somehow we need to untwist our vision of self so that it conforms with reality instead of constantly struggling against it.

[11] Aquinata Böckmann interprets the opprobria of RB 58:7 in terms of a willingness to serve, to accept the status of a servant. See "Seeking God: The Benedictine Way," *Tjurunga* 53 (1997), pp. 5-23.

[12] We who have lived through the decades since the end of Vatican II sometimes forget how massive and immobile monastic life was formerly. No detail of observance could be modified without a great deal of fuss. In fact many of little rituals and customs common in monasteries of the 1950s were already well documented by the twelfth century. They were nearly a thousand years old, giving monasteries an aura of antiquity much beloved by makers of TV documentaries. As an institution monasticism tends in the direction of conservatism. This has its advantages, but it also creates the possibility of becoming hidebound and moribund. Understood wrongly this eighth step of humility can be used as a blunt instrument to legitimate the tyranny of precedent and avoid the challenges which follow attention to conscience, the Spirit at work in the Church and the "signs of the times".

[13] This is the theme of Margaret Mead's book *Culture and Commitment: A Study of the Generation Gap* (London: Granada, 1972.), p. 110: "But whatever stand they take, none of the young, neither the most idealistic nor the most cynical , is untouched by the sense that there are no adults anywhere in the world from whom they can learn what the next steps should be."

[14] *Culture and Commitment*, p. 119.

[15] Hum 42; SBOp 3.48-49.

[16] Apo 23; SBOp 3.100.14.

# X
# RESTRAINT OF SPEECH

The ninth, tenth and eleventh steps of humility have to do with restraint of speech, a topic that Benedict treated at greater length in Chapter 6 of the Rule. Obedience and patience are humility in action, silence is humility in word.[1] It is significant that the word *taciturnitas* (taciturnity or restraint of speech) is used. It is human noise or conversation that Benedict is trying to limit, not environmental noise. He uses the word *silentium* four times: once in relation to meal times and listening to the reading (RB 38.5), once in stating a general principle but with special reference to the period after the final office of Compline (RB 42.1), once about the siesta RB 48.5), and once referring to the recollectedness surrounding the liturgy (RB 52.2). The verb *silere* is used twice, without much emphasis (RB 1.12, 6.1). It is *taciturnitas* and *tacere* that are used in the sixth and seventh chapters to describe what we would term "silence". Restraint of speech is less absolute than silence. The fact that there are sometimes good reasons for abandoning it (RB 42.8, 53.16) does not mean that is not a good principle for monks most of the time.

There is nothing romantic about monastic silence. It is a moral matter more than anything else. If a monastery has a certain aura of peace, it is to be hoped that this derives from the holiness of those who live there, rather than from the fact that it is sitting on an exclusive piece of real estate, furnished and equipped with an eye to atmosphere and able to market itself as a haven of quiet. A noisy world craves silence out of sheer perversity; instead of creating its own it seeks to exploit and consume the silence of others, and then happily returns to its own stridency. Monastic silence is golden because it is a precious distillation of sustained fidelity to grace; it is not a commodity to be admired with a view to easy acquisition. This is as true for the monks themselves as for visitors. Silence is a quality to be acquired by personal discipline, not an external asset whose absence is bewailed and blamed on others.

Silence is related to solitariness.[2] The easiest way to restrict conversation is to be alone. If one cannot be alone then one needs to be with others who also desire a similar measure of silence. This demands a common policy and, probably, structures. A calm environment certainly helps but a silent life needs more than that.

Monastic silence is more than an atmospheric effect or a mindless expression of discipline and order. Silence has as its purpose the promotion of a life of prayer and contemplation. The worth of silence is to be assessed in terms of its suitability for nurturing the interior life. The practice of silence needs to be governed by an awareness of how it can contribute to the contemplative dimension of the monastic day. This can be seen as operating at different levels.

*a) Absence of Noise*

Noise attracts the attention and distracts the mind from its concentration. Any task that requires sensitivity demands the reduction of irrelevant sensory stimulation. Hi-tech "white noise" can help to homogenize ambient sounds into a steady background blur, but traditional monastic discipline and separation work better in protecting the possibility of sustained attention.

### b) Absence of Disturbance

Noise is rarely neutral. Even when it has no content it makes demands on psychic energy. Intrusive sounds batter and violate every cell of the body and make physical quiet more difficult. Usually, however, it is the content or meaning of the sounds that causes the most disturbance. What we hear (or overhear) upsets or excites us. What comes through our ears has the capacity to change our emotions. It follows that if we want to enjoy more freedom from undue emotional upset, some measure of auditory control can help.

### c) Absence of Frivolity

Whether sound brings us joy or sadness it unseats the equilibrium of the heart and makes us, by our changeable moods, a plaything of external events. Instead of being serious and solid people we become insubstantial, ungrounded and flighty. There is no one at home in us except the flickering images we receive from outside.

### d) Absence of Movement

Noise and movement belong together. The effect of noise is to render stillness impossible without an

uncommon degree of personal discipline. The way
we signal disturbance is by movement. People often
find that a previous conversation can make it hard to
sit still during meditation. Needless to say inward
concentration is even more out of the question. No
doubt this is why the Desert Fathers often counselled
their clients to stay in their cells, to renounce
movement and to love stability.

*e) Absence of Restlessness*

The same mobility occurs at the level of
commitment. It is mobility of mind that subverts the
contemplative act and this restlessness is due to
interior division and an inconsistency between ideals
and reality. Although contemplation makes a monk
intent on God and leads him to inward rest and
stillness, it cannot be found except in a heart already
possessed by some measure of quietness.

A listening heart, a quiet mind, a subdued
imagination, stilled passions, a body at rest and a non-
intrusive environment—these form a continuum of
silence that facilitates the soul's attention to God. It is
to provide such conditions that the monastic observance
of silence exists. No doubt the concrete structures
(whether they be, in particular cases, extensive or
minimal) are more favourable for some than for others.
Silence is such an important reality, however, that it
should not be reduced to the common norm. Each one
of us needs to find our own silence. Unless we do, we
will never find our hearts.

~ 56 ~
*The ninth step of humility is*
*that a monk forbids his tongue to speak,*
*restraining his speech*
*and not speaking until an answer is required.*

~ 57 ~
*Scripture shows this:*
*"In much speaking sin is not avoided."*

~ 58 ~
*And:*
*"A talkative person has no direction on earth."*

As a monk moves closer to becoming a perfect disciple (RB 6.3) he discovers his need to take an active stand, and sometimes to make up his mind not to speak. Here it is not a question of an external rule but of a deliberate decision taken by the monk not to break the spell of silence. This means short-circuiting his need to express himself, to communicate, to feel in a state of relatedness to others, to recreate. It means standing more intensely alone, not yielding to the attractions of a moment's relaxation, but keeping intact the creative tension that mindfulness and a purposeful existence involve. Benedict goes further than this in the sixth chapter of the Rule. He judges silence to be such an benefit that sometimes even good and holy words are better omitted (RB 6.1-3).

It is hard for us who come from a culture that prizes verbal proficiency to appreciate this standpoint. Picturing a monk that has progressed well in contemplative prayer, Benedict insists that his remaining in contemplation is of

more ultimate benefit to himself and others than any
words he might utter. With all due respect to the
Dominicans, their motto *Contemplata aliis tradere*,
normally translated "To hand on to others what has
been contemplated" could also be rendered "To betray
to others what has been contemplated". Contemplation
occurs in a non-verbal zone of the human spirit. In so
far as contemplative prayer has content it does not
translate easily into words and concepts; only images
or evocations can adumbrate its reality. The Word is
beyond words. Contemplation brings us so close to God
that God ceases to be a clear object of consciousness.
We are drawn into the divine subjectivity and have no
language to convey the integrity of the experience. We
find it easy to characterize and categorize people we
know slightly. Those whom we love intensely always
defy our powers of description and analysis. A monk
whose life is given fully to contemplation has no
inclination to write a book on contemplation (as I have
done). Mystical prayer is a self-fulfilling and self-
justifying occupation. It leads nowhere else because it
is itself the goal of all other activity, an anticipation—
according to the tradition—of our eternal destiny in
heaven.

It is by approaching restraint of speech through
contemplation that we begin to appreciate why St
Benedict locates it near the summit of the ascent. Silence
is a means by which we can give our full attention to
the Word. It is not seen as an elementary discipline to
be enforced externally. Rather, it is a tendency that
develops in monks as prayer deepens and becomes more
continuous. Another way of stating this is to say that it

is by recollection that the Word received in the liturgy and in *lectio divina* is able to continue speaking to us and provoking our response. Our dialogue with God permeates the day. What is expected of the institution is that it will provide conditions favorable to such a development and allow the possibility of living silently when one has attained the spiritual level which makes it imperative.

Silence is also the means of maintaining that innocence and simplicity of vision that contemplation demands. Much conversation clouds perception. The relentless exchange of information and opinion tends to substitute extensive knowledge for intensity of experience. Many things may be cognitively familiar but not at any great depth. The quiz champion and the purveyors of facts are rarely philosophers. On the other hand, an attraction to contemplative prayer often carries with it a willingness to channel one's energies, to specialize, to pursue the one thing necessary rather than be fragmented by the pursuit of multiplicity.[3] It is impossible to make much progress without a fairly radical renunciation. In this context the reduction of speech seems reasonable.

There is another angle familiar to readers of St James' Epistle. Speech is the commonest source of sin for people trying to live good lives. It is as though they compensate for the discipline and deprivation of virtuous living through uncontrolled conversation. Benedict forbids murder (RB 4.3) and most monasteries frown on monks literally stabbing one other in the back. The same effect, however, can often be achieved in a socially acceptable form by strategic and self-righteous calumny or detraction. Likewise those that love contention (See

RB 4.68) can upset others' peace and acceptance by attempting to make trouble by murmuring. This is a reality with which Benedict was familiar and against which he made a strong stand (See RB 4.39, 5.14, 5.17, 5.18, 5.19, 23.1, 34.6, 35.13, 40.8, 41.5, 53.18). Speech can be malicious or contentious; it can also be a criminal waste of time and energy, and a distraction that prevents monks from attaining their goal. Through aimless conversation fervor is lost, morale undermined and many unconscious and uncreative forces are set in play. This is the point of Benedict's quotation from Ps 139:12: "A talkative person has no direction on earth." Even when the content of conversation is overtly harmless, a lot of time can be lost and any sense of direction in life is eroded.

It is naive to think that our conversation needs little vigilance, that it can be left alone to find its own level. Unless our speech is subordinate to our fundamental purpose in life it will imperceptibly subvert our efforts. To the extent that our hearts remain divided, we will often find—to our shame—that our spontaneous speech sides with the part of us that resists grace. The witness of so many masters of spiritual life in different traditions is constant. We are wasting our time in spiritual endeavor if we do not take steps to monitor our conversation and ensure that it does not erode our integrity and destroy what we are trying to promote. If we examine our conscience rigorously we will probably find that many of our daily sins (including sins of omission) are triggered by or expressed in conversation. Add to this its effect on our fluctuating moods and we may well conclude that this area might need more attention than we hitherto suspected.

Silence becomes progressively more important. In the early days of monastic life it is mainly a question of personal discipline and respect for others (RB Prol 47). It is true that the imagination and feelings are still easily aroused by conversation, but it is not always clear that this susceptibility is rendered safe by more silence. There are other channels of stimulation and distraction: reading, fantasy, memory. In the beginning, because there is a fair amount of inner havoc, a few conversations more or less may make little difference. They may even be helpful if they have the effect of breaking the tyranny of obsessive thoughts and serve the purpose of keeping the newcomer in touch with the real world.[4] Silence is much more crucial at a later stage. When the mind and heart have become purified and integrated so that prayer comes readily, infidelity to silence can cause more damage. It is much more a deliberate choice, because the capacity for prayer has been given; it is in turning away from this gift that the monk reveals his baser priorities. Symbolically speaking, it is a substantial act of rebellion, a rejection of grace offered. In the first place the mature monk soon learns by sorry experience that talking often destroys the heart's receptivity of prayer and of God. It gives an engaged signal. Secondly, because the content of conversation is often uncharitable, the purity of the heart's intent is soiled by an overt denial of love. The quality of prayer, when it happens, deteriorates. Thirdly, in turning from prayer to unprofitable conversation, the monk is reversing the fundamental choice inherent in his vocation. Such a radical denial of what is most precious cannot but leave a sour aftertaste.

If silence is such a priority for monks and nuns, perhaps this involves a certain counter-cultural stance with regard to domestic administration. In the interests of good communication within the community, many monasteries insist on meetings, discussions and negotiation as an ordinary part of monastic life. It is worth asking whether it would be possible to adopt a policy of keeping such affrays at a minimum in the interests of monastic *quies*. This would involve a considerable change in attitude. Perhaps there are those who have progressed to the point where they are minding their own business, delegating decisions to those most qualified to take them and being tolerant of others' peculiarities. It would mean that their spiritual life has developed to the extent that they do not get too upset by minor happenings around them. Obviously, such a method of administration will not suit everyone and it could easily lead to abuses. At the same time it needs to be stated that silence is violated not only by frivolous chatting but also by serious (and especially divisive) discussion. To eliminate one and promote the other seems pointless. As St Benedict notes, there is scope for refraining from talking even about good things (RB 6.2-3). To be serious about fidelity to the priority of prayer requires that many alternative activities be left aside.

Up to his point we have been discussing the violation of silence in terms of conversation with others. Sometimes monastic communities manage to keep the rule of silence while subverting its purpose. The use of sign-language, common from the Middle Ages, was still customary when I was a young monk. It was a time-consuming and inefficient mode of communication that was perilously prone to misunderstanding and unable to encompass the subtlety necessary in delicate situations. Perhaps, also, we need to address the topic of communicating with other community-members via notes. This functional manner of transferring information without human contact has become customary in many communities who see themselves as dedicated to silence. It fails in so far as it circumvents the face-to-face encounter of direct speech and the awareness of another's reaction or response. It may seem business-like, but at the level of common humanity it must be judged defective.

We must also include in our reflections the effects of radio, television and the Internet. Using them often represents no meeting of minds but a unilateral exposure of oneself to indoctrination by the mass media or individual opinions. We need to be aware of the content and bias of what we thus passively absorb. Thomas Merton regarded television as an inauthentic substitute for contemplation.[5] The passivity that opens us to formation by the Spirit also allows us to be manipulated. It is highly unlikely that evangelical distinctiveness of thought and action will be strengthened by the mass media. Orwell's *1984* is a reminder that control of the media is a powerful instrument of repression, whether we know it or not. Television programs are usually slanted. Newspapers undoubtedly contain, in addition to a substantial quantity of mere entertainment, not only news but views. Who knows the effects on personal values and standards that rub off from popular music? It seems obvious that the development of an authentic contemplative life ordinarily needs zones of silence. Monasteries generally provide these and most people who are serious about prayer eventually get to the point of securing possibilities of quiet. If, because contemplation is slow in coming, we fill the spaces with electronic entertainment and information, then contemplation will never come. If we insistently negate the void, then the void cannot produce its effects in us.

The impression that the older monastic sources give is that there is barely any scope for conversation in monastic life. This is because speech-related benefits are so obvious and immediate that they are rarely mentioned. Most monks know by experience how they have been helped by good teaching, sound advice, fraternal support and even light-hearted diversion. Laws and exhortations are not needed to sell such good practices. Bernard of Clairvaux is an exception to the rule when he states explicitly: "There is great utility in speaking and frequently most valuable fruit is found in the tongue".[6] The advantages of silence, on the other hand, easily go unremarked. They need to be actively promoted if they are not to be ignored. When we read these ancient texts nowadays, we may need to keep reminding ourselves of the human context to which the writings were addressed. They are not appeals for absolute silence but efforts to induce monks to limit their conversation to what is appropriate to their way of life and stage of progress.

There are three forms of conversation that are especially abhorrent to St Benedict. These can be seen in the stern conclusion to his chapter on silence. Here he rejects whatever is unseemly, useless or provokes laughter. The three cases are not quite the same and should be treated separately.

## a) Scurrility

The word *scurrilitas* used by St Benedict in RB 6.8 comes from the word *scurra* which usually means a clown, jester or buffoon.[7] Probably the most significant problem with such people is that they were, by nature, outsiders. The conduct typical of them was to poke fun at the conventions and pretensions of the group on whose margins they lived, to point out when the emperor had no clothes. In a society that lacked constitutional law this inbuilt exercise of *lèse-majesté* was an important function; it served to relativize an absolute supremacy. A monastery is somewhat different. Benedict was aware of the political import of humor. Mockery easily undermines the honor of persons and the credibility of structures, the foundations on which a monastic community depends. It is the opposite of that grave sense of reverence that Benedict often inculcates. Flippancy and fun are often thin disguises for cynicism and disillusionment. They can assume an edge of mordancy that seeks to wound others and make them ridiculous. Even when such sallies are "harmless" and have no local target, they tend to erode community standards and to bring into disrepute persons and values that deserve better. A certain line of sexual jokes can, for example, give a very ambiguous message regarding the values of celibacy or chastity and cumulatively make it more difficult for some to arrive at personal integration in the area of sexuality. Having said this, I should add that repression, prudishness and primness are equally destructive. Most of us would prefer to live in a community that is free of gross vulgarity, but too much emphasis on refinement can lead to elitism. Benedictine monks should always keep their feet on the ground; *humus* and humility are, after all, etymologically connected. Becoming too ethereal leads to problems. Perhaps this is why Benedict, having damned *scurrilitates* to eternal exclusion, mildly suggests that monks might reduce the level of their *scurrilitates* as an optional extra for Lent (RB 49.7). Notwithstanding the idyllic image of ancient Clairvaux, Bernard deplored the level of "frivolous thoughts, idle chatter, jokes and coarse stories" in his monastery,[8] even though he himself could be funny and indelicate (according to our standards) and was a good friend of Burchard of Balerne who wrote a totally frivolous treatise on monastic beards.[9] As Benedict himself remarks in a different context, "everything in due measure" (RB 31.12, 48.9).

### b) Unprofitable Talk

The expression used in *RB 1980* is "gossip". This is not exactly what Benedict says although gossip is one species of idle talk. What is here reprobated is pleasant, aimless chit-chat that fills the time and is mildly entertaining. Its principle characteristic is its vacuous-ness.[10] The Latin word *otium* is ambiguous. It can refer either to leisure or idleness. This leads to difficulties. Thus, for example, there is a place for contemplative leisure in the monastic day,[11] whereas idleness is the enemy of the soul, consuming time both for work and for *lectio divina* (RB 48.1). Talk is idle when it displaces other useful occupations; it is part of the ancient monastic aberration that was given the name "acedia". It is in the area of time-usage that a monk faces a very specific challenge. Time and opportunity for prayer are given him; yet there is the constant temptation either to use the time available for other pursuits or to make that time useless by a failure to keep guard over heart, mind and emotions.[12] An excess of escapist conversation quickly torpedoes any chance of growth in prayerfulness. Another word Benedict uses for light conversation is *fabula*, and he twice reprobates such activity (RB 43.8, 48.18).

### c) Talk Leading to Laughter

This obviously includes jokes and funny stories. This is the least defensible of Benedict's prohibitions. Presumably Benedict would see this as degrading the standard of observance in the community, abusing time and filling the mind with useless and harmful thoughts. On this last effect of humorous conversation, Cassian remarks through Abba Isaac:

> The mind is shaped during its prayer by what it was beforehand. When we prostrate ourselves in prayer, our previous actions, words and impressions continue to play before the minds of our imagination, just as they did before, making us angry or sad, or causing us to relive past lusts or foolish laughter. I am ashamed to say that we are even entertained by comic words and deeds and our mind is diverted by recalling conversations we have had.[13]

While taking the point that excessive laughter is unmonastic, we need to remember that gloom is even more destructive of the monastic ideal. Undoubtedly Benedict was not a clown. He seems to have been a man who was sober, phlegmatic and even a little dour. His failure to appreciate humor may have been the result of a personal blind spot or a cultural trait. We do not have to agree with him unreservedly. It is sufficient to hear what he is saying, to allow ourselves to be influenced and then to decide what is appropriate monastic conduct in our own particular situation. Nobody wants monks to spend their days braying like donkeys or giggling like adolescents. But, as we have already suggested, before attaining such a level of excess there is scope for humour which is moderate and kind, if its effects are agglutinative rather than divisive.

Although speech is often good and serves as a means of helping one another, it is not a sacrament. There is sometimes a problem with people in positions of power who think their every word is golden. Occasionally one gets the impression that some suppose that all issues can be resolved by talking. There are persons with problems who think this; there are also those whom they consult who believe it. Non-stop talking can be a means of insulating oneself from the shock of the real. A time for speaking there certainly is, but there is also a time for refraining from further discussion. After a full and frank disclosure with genuine listening on both sides, a quiet and solitary interval is needed both for prayer and for cherishing the otherness and challenge of what one has heard. Each party in the sharing should be more concerned with appreciating what was given by the other rather than merely replaying their own words. The discipline of restraint of speech is sometimes a necessary factor in making conversation fruitful. Often it is in silence and solitude that a true solution to problems is found. It is in quiet pondering that we discover our need for God to save; we become aware of the extent of our poverty and our lack of capabilities to deal with the situation. In our own life we will not make progress until we accept our utter indigence. In helping others, likewise, we will soon come to the end of our resourcefulness and feel obliged to fall back on prayer (RB 28.3-5).

If speech can be good, silence can be bad. This being so, the rules which govern the monastic observance of silence must be considered as having merely relative value. Bernard of Clairvaux was aware that rules of silence make it difficult for monks to render the help and counsel they owe their brothers,[14] and can allow misunderstandings to be perpetuated.[15] Indeed, the excessive structures of consultation and communication found in some monasteries are probably a reaction to the destructive effects of too rigid rules of silence. Obviously the golden mean is the best solution.

External silence unsupported by personal desire can lead to riotous imaginations. Underneath a recollected facade can be a mind that is, to use an old phrase, the devil's playground. Plunging someone into silence will usually produce good effects only if that person wants silence, has an attraction for prayer and has some skills to pass the time profitably. Too much silence too early in spiritual progress exposes the person to the possibility of being swamped by unconscious agenda before the development of an infrastructure to handle it.

Benedict regards talkativeness as something that inhibits our capacity to receive salvation. Excessive conversation expresses and reinforces a lack of personal discipline in our life. It restricts our capacity to listen, it banishes mindfulness and opens the door to distraction and escapism. Talking too much often convinces us of the correctness of our own conclusions and leads some into thinking they are wise. It can be a subtle exercise in arrogance and superiority. Often patterns of dependence, manipulation and dominance are established and maintained by the medium of speech. A conversation has many hidden dynamics and cannot always be assayed by reading a transcript. Whatever its content, however, Benedict has severe reservations about the ultimate utility of any talking that does not match the description he gives in the eleventh step of humility: brief, serious and reasonable.

The main point to carry from these reflections is that restraint of speech is a nuanced value, not something to be maximally recommended to all. We need to think in terms of silence as an ascetical practice instead of concentrating on rules and external structures of silence. If we are to listen to St Benedict and the whole monastic tradition, then we need to allow ourselves to be challenged in our daily practice. The fact that most of us will fall short of what Benedict seems to be proposing as an ideal is no excuse for eliminating silence from our personal inventory of values. I doubt that there is anyone on earth who could not profit from being a little less uncontrolled in their speech. Even abstracting from the quality of our conversation, I think many of us would be much better off if we did not speak as much as we do.

~ 59 ~
*The tenth step of humility is
that the monk is not ready and prompt to laugh,
for it is written:
"A fool lifts up his voice in laughter."*

The shortest of the steps of humility is not very popular.[16] Scholastic philosophy saw laughter as the most distinctive human activity, present in every human culture yet denied to both angels and animals. Benedict and the Master seem to regard it as a major vice. Nor is this particular verse a slip of the pen, since Benedict underlines the same point in 4.53-54 and has an even fiercer denunciation of laughter in 6.8:

> We damn to an eternal exclusion in all places *scurrilitates*, idle words and talk that causes laughter, and we do not permit a disciple to open his mouth for such kind of talk.

The Latin *aeterna clausura...damnamus* is stronger than most translations indicate. Although it is taken directly from RM 9.51 this verse represents an uncharacteristically severe admonition.

We have already discussed some aspects of this question in reflecting on the ninth degree of humility. There is not much more to be said. It is probably true that laughter was a symbolic gesture that contradicted the whole tenor of monastic life as Benedict understood it. Laughter undermines seriousness, mindfulness, diligence, sobriety, moderation and kindness and acceptance of others. Loud laughter evokes a lifestyle more typical of gyrovagues (RB 1.11) than of the stolid, stable monks that Benedict cherished.

Perhaps this step of humility needs to be interpreted in the light of the Beatitudes. In that case laughter and rejoicing belong to the next life; here below the lot of Christians is that salutary sadness which went by the Greek term *penthos*.[17] Even in that context, a life without laughter is a very lofty ideal and presupposes a level of spiritual intensity that few experience and none can claim as an habitual reality in their lives. We know that the saints laughed, as do many people who have been icons of Christ in our lives. Think of how much good was done by the smiling popes, John XXIII and John Paul I. Apart from patently unwholesome outbursts that stem from some inner frenzy or are associated with mockery, unkindness or political division, there is probably no harm in postponing a campaign to eliminate laughter until some of our more significant vices have been curtailed.

~ 60 ~
*The eleventh step of humility is*
*that when a monk speaks*
*he does so mildly and without laughter,*
*humbly, with gravity and in a few reasonable words.*
*He does not speak in a loud voice.*

~ 61 ~
*As it is written:*
*"The wise are known for their few words."*

When Pope Paul VI visited Monte Cassino in
October 1964 he called attention to a certain "elegant
gravity" of style which typified the sons and daughters
of St Benedict.[18] The idea of *gravitas* as a virtue
associated with humility and silence occurs six times in
the Rule (RB 6.3, 7.60, 22.6, 42.11, 43.2, 47.4). Benedict
probably intended more than a certain stateliness of gait
and demeanor. For him gravity was a sign of a solid
monk: one who weighs his words and eschews whatever
lacks substance. The translation given in *RB 1980* is
"becoming modesty"; it conveys something of the
meaning of the word, but it needs to be nuanced.

The key to understanding this step of humility is
to appreciate that Benedict is itemizing the qualities of
an elderly person who has attained a measure of
wisdom: gentle, serious, humble, grave, taciturn, low-
voiced and sparing of words. There is no hint of
brashness, assertiveness, initiative, color, verve or
panache. Benedict is offering the same advice as most
proponents of wisdom. He is telling the young to
emulate the qualities that come unbidden along with
white hair and arthritic limbs.[19] A timely exhortation,
no doubt, but one that is a little unfair. It would be a
wonderful world if younger people had all the qualities
that come with sustained effort and experience, but it is
delusional to believe that it could ever happen. In all
probability they will never arrive at such mellowness if
we do not encourage them first of all to act their age and

exhibit the qualities of youth: brashness, assertiveness, initiative, colour, verve and panache. And let them make mistakes; there is no better school of maturity. If we want to harness the energy and drive of pre-geriatrics, then we must be prepared to put up with a little abrasiveness. There is no point in trying to fight against the slowness of authentic growth. Most people will soften over the next 40 years. St Benedict reminds us not to be so zealous in scraping off the rust that we end up ruining what is underneath (RB 64.12). Meanwhile it is worth recalling a saying of Augustine: "Let us not forget what we were once, and then we will not lose hope for those who are now what we used to be."[20]

It needs to be reiterated; the eleventh step of humility is to be expected only at the eleventh hour. It is not a code of monastic etiquette to be forced on newcomers, but the normal outcome of a lifetime spent in search of wisdom. What Benedict presents in this eleventh step is the external form of one who has made much progress in prayer. Without the inner substance the humble exterior is a sham. If we follow the lead of the Sermon on the Mount and St Benedict's teaching, we will soon move away from all manner of play-acting and allow truth to serve as the pervasive principle of all we do. Then, with God's help, we will arrive at the summit of humility. And, as soon as we open our mouths, our solid wisdom will be apparent to all— except ourselves.

## Notes

[1] "Just as in the domain of action, humility expresses itself positively by obedience, so in the domain of the word, humility consists in the negative and restrictive effort involved in restraint of speech." Translated from Adalbert de Vogüé, *La Règle de Saint Benoît*, IV (SChr 184; Paris: Cerf, 1971), pp. 265.

[2] See M. Casey, "Solitariness," *Tjurunga*, 33 (1987), pp. 3-23. "The Dialectic of Solitude and Communion in Cistercian Communities," *CSQ* 21.4 (1988), pp. 273-309. "In communi vita fratrum: St Bernard's Teaching on Cenobitic Solitude," *ASOC* 46 (1990), pp. 243-261.

[3] A classic expression of this theme is to be found in the account of Benedict's life given in the second book of Gregory the Great's *Dialogues*: "Turning his back on the study of literature, [Benedict], after leaving his father's house and property, desired to please only God and sought the habit of monasticism. Therefore he withdrew, knowingly ignorant, and wisely uneducated *scienter nescius et sapienter indoctus*." (2.1; SChr 260, p. 126.)

[4] Light conversations also serve to establish an infrastructure of communication and trust without which more significant dialogue becomes more difficult to achieve. This is the area of the "meta-message"—where conversation is seen as modifying the relationship as well as transmitting information.

[5] For a typical diatribe, see "Inner Experience: Notes on Contemplation (VII)," *CSQ* 19 (1984), pp. 269-270: "The life of the television-watcher is a kind of caricature of contemplation. Passivity, uncritical absorption, receptivity, inertia. Not only that, but a gradual progressive yielding to the mystic attraction until one is spellbound in a state of complete union. The trouble with this caricature is that it is really the exact opposite of contemplation: for true contemplation is precisely the fruit of a most active and intransigent rupture with all the captivates the senses, the emotions, and the will

on a material or temporal level....The other, the ersatz, is the nadir of intellectual and emotional slavery."

[6] De Diversis 17.7; SBOp 6a.155.5-6. Much of this sermon concerns the text, "In much speaking you will not avoid sin." In a remarkably even-handed treatment he adds to his warnings against evil speech, the equally serious admonition not to inhibit life-giving and edifying words.

[7] Others to whom the term was attributed were the smart young men on society's fringes, the wandering scholars of the middle ages and those of low rank and coarse conduct. For further suggestions see Philip B. Corbett, "Unidentified Source-Material Common to Regula Magistri, Regula Benedicti and Regula IV Patrum," *RBS* 5 (1977), pp. 27-31.

[8] Humb 8, SBOp 5.447.6. In his recommendations for Lent he says to his monks: "let the ear fast from its evil itch to listen to stories and rumors and whatever is unprofitable and has little bearing on salvation. Let the tongue fast from detraction and murmuring, from useless, vain and scurrilous words and indeed sometimes—on account of the seriousness of silence—from words that could seem necessary. Let the hand fast from unprofitable sign-making." Quad 3.4; SBOp 4.367.9-14. The fact that Bernard recommends abstention from such species of communication during Lent seems to indicate that they were not uncommon in ordinary time.

[9] Burchardus de Bellevaux, *Apologia de barbis* (Cambridge University Press, 1935).

[10] T. S. Eliot parodied this kind of conversation in *The Cocktail Party* (London: Faber and Faber, 1950.)

[11] See Jean Leclercq, *Otia Monastica: Études sur le vocabulaire de contemplation au moyen âge* (Studia Anselmiana #51; Rome, Herder, 1965.)

[12] As William of St Thierry notes in his *Golden Epistle*, #82: "It is ridiculous to devote time to idle pursuits as a means of avoiding idleness." (SChr 223, p. 206).)

[13] Cassian, *Conference* 9.3; SChr 54, p. 42.

[14] Adv 3.5; SBOp 4.178-179.

[15] SC 29.4; SBOp 1.206.3-6.

[16] For a full treatment of this topic see Pedro Max Alexander OSB, "La prohibición de la risa en la Regula Benedicti: Intento de explicación e interpretación," *RBS* 5 (1977), pp. 225-283.Irven M. Resnick, "'Risus Monasticus': Laughter and Medieval Monastic Culture," *Revue Bénédictine* 97 (1987), pp. 90-100. For a reminder of some of the issues involved in interpreting more difficult passages, see M. Casey, "The Hard Sayings of the Rule of Benedict," *Tjurunga* 3 (1972), pp. 133-143.

[17] See Irénée Hausherr, Penthos: The *Doctrine of Compunction in the Christian East* (CS 53; Kalamazoo; Cistercian Publications, 1982.) This is a translation of a classic work originally published in 1944.

[18] Discourse "Quale saluto", translated in *The Pope Speaks* 10 (1965), pp. 120-126.

[19] Another example: St. Augustine notes that approaching old age is a great ally for those who have had some success in the struggle against the tyranny of carnal concupiscence. *De Nuptiis et Concupiscentia* 1.25.28; PL 44, 430b.

[20] *On the Psalms* 50.24; CCL38, p. 615.

# XI
# INTEGRATION
# AND
# TRANSFORMATION

And so we clamber up to the final step on the ladder of lowliness. What Benedict describes here can first be summarized under the heading of integration. It is the coming together of all the facets of the monk's complex existence that will soon lead to his transformation—the restoration of God's likeness within. In contrast to the diriment fragmentation that follows narcissism of thought and deed, humility causes the harmonious flowering of all that is good and beautiful, as much in the order of creation as in the sphere of grace. There is no longer conflict between intention and performance, inner and outer, human and divine. All the disparate energies of human being now flow in a single unified torrent. No longer weakened by division and dispersion, the monk lives a life of concentrated union with God. The *intentio cordis* which Benedict cites as the distinguishing quality of deep prayer is no longer a transient experience but is near to becoming the ordinary state in which the monk lives.[1] This is the state envisaged by the ancient monastic emphasis on purity of heart.

Let us examine the description of the perfect monk as conceived by Benedict and the Master. It may, at first glance, seem negative but it portrays a man no longer secretly struggling against his noblest aspirations, one totally submissive to grace. Paradoxically his spiritual attainment is signalled most effectively by his attitude to his own negativity. In accepting the unconditioned love of God he also accepts his own unworthiness. He does not fear to gaze into the depths of his own indigence; instead he allows himself to be permeated by the truth of his own earth-generated existence. The sort of humility he acts out is, in fact, an exaltation of God's gratuitous love for human beings—even while they remain sinners.

*~ 62 ~*
*The twelfth step of humility is that*
*in his body as well as in his heart*
*a monk always manifests humility to those who see him.*


*~ 63 ~*
*That is true at the Work of God,*
*in the oratory, the monastery the garden,*
*on a journey, in the fields, or anywhere else.*
*Whether he sits, walks or stands,*
*his head is to be always bowed and his eyes fixed on the*
*earth.*


*~ 64 ~*
*At every hour,*
*regarding himself as guilty because of his sins,*
*let him consider himself already*
*at the fearful judgement of God.*

*~ 65 ~*
*Let him always say in his heart*
*what the publican in the Gospel said, his eyes fixed on the*
*earth:*
*"Lord, I am a sinner.*
*I am not worthy to raise my eyes to heaven."*


*~ 66 ~*
*And with the Prophet:*
*"I am bent over and humbled in every way."*


The integration presented by Benedict is not high integration—the monk transfigured into some species of superior being. No, it is low integration. The monk is wedded to his earthliness, and rid of the pervasive temptation to get above himself. One who walks the way of lowliness is something of an anti-hero. There is no trace of what Thomas Merton has called "Promethean virtue"[2] here. The Christian saint remains one of us, without glamor or high reputation. "He had no form or grace to draw our gaze, no beauty to attract our desire. He was despised and rejected, a man of sorrows, no stranger to grief" (Is 53:3). Even at the summit of the spiritual ascent there is no escaping the cross of Christ. What has changed is that the monk has learned by experience to stop kicking against the goad. He has begun to accept that God is present even in the most unpalatable of human experiences, and his search for God is no longer postponed by ill-advised campaigns to improve his temporal lot.

It is important to realize that spiritual progress brings no guarantee of temporal fringe-benefits. In *Inner*

*Experience* Thomas Merton quotes a Zen poem which describes enlightenment.

> Devoid of thought, I sat quietly
> by the desk in my official room,
> with my fountain-mind undisturbed,
> as serene as water;
> a sudden crash of thunder,
> the mind doors burst open,
> and lo, there sits an old man
> in all his homeliness.[3]

What this text seems to intimate is that even the most spectacular spiritual experience leaves the external condition of life intact. The figure we observe is far from being a radiant post-enlightenment visionary, it is simply a homely old man comfortably sitting in his chair gazing placidly into the twilight. Contemplative experience roots persons more deeply in humility. Although such experience is something of a preview of heaven, its effect is to render loveable, in those who have it, the things of earth. It does not take away from them their ordinariness, nor does it act as insulation from their own liabilities or from the ravages of others. If anything, it permits them to experience these negativities more pungently. Even stranger, it leaves them morally fragile, like the rest of the human race. Their will adheres closely to the absolute Good, but elements of unruliness remain at other levels of being.

We have been brainwashed by hagiographical excess into believing that sanctity involves the removal of all irritants and faults. The saint is one with no bad

habits or annoying quirks, who sings in tune, is entirely
without prejudice and is astonishingly wise in every
department of human endeavor. Alas, such is not the
case. Saints can be as narrow and cranky as the rest of
us. What constitutes their sainthood is the truth of their
relationships with God and with neighbor. To begin
with, biology and personal history cannot be changed.
Blemishes of character, blind spots, faults and wrong
actions remain as reminders that even the greatest saints
are closer to us sinners than to God. The difference
between us and them is that they are fully aware of their
own fragility; we judge ourselves to be sturdier than we
are. The monk who has attained the twelfth step of
humility is under no illusions: he does not wish to be
called holy prematurely (RB 4.62). He feels in his bones
that no one is confirmed in virtue this side of the grave.
He is at home with his limitations and so he is content
to number himself among those who rely on the mercy
of God.

If it is the mercy of God that is his song, then the
remembrance of his own malign misdeeds is grist for
his mill. That God should have showered grace on one
so clearly undeserving is a thought that brings much
consolation. There are parallels between the first step
of humility and the last. Both use expressions like
"always" and "at every hour" to emphasize the theme
that the monk should be constantly mindful both of
sin and of God. Yet there are differences. At the
beginning mindfulness is the result of effort. The monk
actively tries to avoid escaping into forgetfulness of
ultimate realities by injecting appropriate thoughts into
awareness. At the end no effort is needed: mindfulness

is second nature. The monk is filled with an awareness of God's love that is totally penetrating. It is nothing like slick theological clichés loosely attached to the surface of the mind and liable to spill out in glib aphorisms and correct ideology. This is a matter of someone for whom divine realities have a certain immediacy. So complete is this consciousness of being loved by God, that it revels in demonstrating the divine gratuity, by feeding on the sense of one's utter unworthiness. No longer is it a question of remembering one's weaknesses in order to avoid being trapped by them. Now the thought of handicaps is a source of joy and comfort; despite so many liabilities God's love has not wavered. Every problem and sin becomes a song of praise for a love that is undeterred by human weakness, blindness or malice.

So pleasant is this thought that it accompanies the monk wherever he goes. Not only in the liturgy or at prayer but travelling or at work in the fields. Mindfulness of God becomes radically independent of techniques. In the spirit of RB 19-20, his whole being is possessed by a deep reverence. No matter where the monk is or what he is doing, he stands in the presence of God. Certainly he is mindful of his past sins and present frailty, but this is mere counterpoint to the dominant melody of divine love. In fact anyone who has arrived at this level of humility will be so liberated from narcissism that any thought of self could be entertained only in function of remembrance of God. In the language used by Bernard of Clairvaux, he begins to love himself only for God's sake.

> Happy are they who deserve to reach the fourth level [of love] where persons love themselves only on account of God. Your righteousness, O God, is like the divine mountains. Love is such a mountain and God's mountain is lofty. Truly this is a rich and luscious mountain. Who will ascend this mountain of the Lord? Who will give me the wings of a dove to fly there and rest? For God's place is in peace and his dwelling is in Sion. Alas for me that my exile has been prolonged. When can flesh and blood, the clay vessel of earthly dwelling, attain to this? When will such a feeling be experienced that the soul, intoxicated by divine love forgets itself that it becomes like a broken vessel, and casts itself wholly into God and adhering to God becomes one spirit with him.[4]

When the self becomes invisible it is rendered totally transparent; it no longer draws attention away from God. Since the will is undividedly conformed to God, only the constraints of spatio-temporal existence now separate faith from vision. Gratitude to God seasoned by a generalized repentance for past selfishness become the principal themes of reflection on life.[5]

We can deduce that the steps of humility are also steps of prayer. All these years the monk has been making progress in the task of building his life around the prayer of the publican that was so praised by Jesus (Lk 18:9-14). The monk described by Benedict is very close to the ideal promulgated in the Eastern Church and in such works as *The Way of the Pilgrim*, in which

the saying of the "Jesus Prayer" is not only the principal
devotional exercise but progressively becomes the theme
song of one's whole life. Humility is a fundamental
element of one's relationship with God; to a large extent
the measure of humility is also the measure of one's
prayer. Without the experience that forces a monk to
lower his estimation of his own merits there is no chance
that he will ever become a contemplative.

St Benedict expects humility to overflow from
within and to stamp its character on the monk's personal
style. The body thus cedes its autonomy to the spirit
and becomes the expression of what is interiorly
experienced. This is a sharp reminder of how utterly
convinced were the ancient monks that body and spirit
were meant to work together. The Cistercians of the
twelfth century saw in the upper reaches of spiritual
life the gradual restoration of the divine likeness not
only inwardly but also visibly in the transformation of
the body. They found it impossible to believe that
inward beauty would not find physical expression,
especially through the face. Just as inner division and
anxiety are mirrored on the countenance, so harmony,
once established within, progressively manifests itself
in the radiant tranquillity of the holy person's face.

In the light of the next section, we must interpret
the bodily manifestation of humility, as described by St
Benedict, as a positive reality. The description itself reads
negatively: in dread of judgement with downcast eyes
and head bowed. To see no more than this external
picture would be to make a mockery of Christ's promise
of a hundredfold—as we can learn from observing the
lives of those who have reached this point. The fruit of

a lifetime's faithful effort must be more than misery. I think that what Benedict means here is that "humility" becomes the total and undisputed determinant of attitudes and actions. The superficial self has almost disappeared. The authentic, inner self has become paramount and, as a result, disorder is banished and truth and love have proportionately more influence on outlook and behaviour. In other words, the monk's life has been radically transformed.

~ 67 ~

*Now, therefore, after ascending all these steps of humility,*
*the monk will quickly arrive*
*at that perfect love of God which casts out fear.*

~ 68 ~

*Through this love,*
*all that he used to observe somewhat fearfully*
*he will now begin to fulfill without effort,*
*as though naturally, from habit.*

~ 69 ~

*[He will act] no longer out of fear of hell,*
*but out of love for Christ,*
*from good habit itself and delight in virtue.*

The steps of the ladder of lowliness lead to a beautiful and serene conclusion. The austere beginnings of monastic life and the subsequent decades of sustained self-renunciation begin, by God's grace, to produce fruit, even in the present life. St Benedict has lopped off the finale of the Master's chapter on humility (RM 10.92-120). Perhaps he did this because it seemed to postpone the profits of humility until heaven, whereas Benedict knew by experience that God delivers on the hundredfold promised by Jesus, and that this abundance of life is worth waiting for. Bernard of Clairvaux also was aware that in the upper reaches of the spiritual life the frontiers between time and eternity are semi-permeable and difficult to define. To the one who experiences it, it seems that heaven begins on earth, though the disproportion between this world and the next remains. It seems that St Benedict sees the process of divinization as attaining a measure of visibility this side of the grave.

In the Rule of Benedict we find added to the end of the Master's text of the Prologue, a few verses that parallel the block we are examining. Both have something to say about the developmental dynamics of monastic life. Benedict recognizes that newcomers will find many aspects of monastic life unpalatable: its entrance is narrow but within will be found freedom and joy, the "cloistral paradise" of which the medieval monks sang.

*~ Prologue 49 ~*
*But as we progress in monasticity (conversatio)*
*and in faith*
*we shall run on the path of God's commandments,*
*our hearts enlarged*
*with the inexpressible delight of love.*

The elements of authentic monastic growth are clearly indicated in this brief text.

*a) Progress in Monasticity*

Monastic life can be very alienating in its early or middle years, depending on individual temperaments. To make progress in *conversatio* is to feel at home in a particular monastery, to have internalized the principal values of monastic life and to have built up an identity in which monasticity is an essential element. This does not happen overnight or without struggle and backsliding. And such progress is never irreversible. But most monks who live content and fruitful lives pass a point beyond which their monastic vocation seems more like a good thing than a bane.

*b) Progress in Faith*

Although not much has been said in these reflections about the theological virtue of faith, it is important to state that faith is the soul of monastic life and of humility. It follows that many difficulties are due to defective faith. It is only the consolation stemming from faith in God's love and fidelity that keeps us going in times of adversity. It is the boldness of faith that teaches us to trust human beings and so escape from the sinful isolation to which we condemn ourselves. It is the revelation of a love that belongs to another sphere that makes it possible for us to accept simultaneously our own unworthiness and the unconditional esteem in which God holds us. It is progress in faith that makes humility possible.

*c) Extending the Capacity to Love*

We fail in love because our hearts are narrow. It is not a dearth of objects for our affection that causes us to remain loveless but a deadness or incapacity on our part. There is a need for healing and freeing. Probably it is only the experience of being loved by God and by other human beings that will effect this change. So the community needs to provide not only ample opportunity for prayer but also abundant evidence of friendship and affection—the "most fervent love" about which St Benedict speaks in RB 72.3. It is love alone that satisfies simultaneously the demands of the Law and the needs of the human heart.[6]

### d) Delight

We have already mentioned the Augustinian theme of *delectatio*. Our relationship with God is coloured mainly by God's desire to give us good things (Lk 11.13). As we unravel the tangled strands of human subjectivity we become more adept at appreciating the giftedness in which we live. Instead of focusing on what goes wrong and wasting time in assigning blame, we become more open to delight in all that is beautiful, willing to be swept toward God on a torrent of gratitude. Spiritual progress is mainly demonstrated by a capacity to find joy in the Lord. The monk begins to be transfigured by his exposure to the divinizing light, *deificum lumen*, of which St Benedict speaks in the Prologue (vs.9).

### e) Energy

As we get older our natural reserves of enthusiasm, verve and resilience begin to decline; there have been so many disappointments and frustrations that the noonday (or mid-life) devil of acedia finds us willing prey. Parallel to this predictable, calendar-related energy crisis is a surprising surge in vitality that stems from a spiritual liveliness. "And while our outward humanity wastes away, our interior humanity is being renewed day after day" (2 Cor 4.6). No longer is it enough to walk in the way of the Lord's command-ments. We run. "Though youths faint and are weary and the young drop exhausted, those who hope in the Lord will renew their strength, they will fly on eagles' wings. They will run unwearied, walk without becoming tired" (Is 40:30-31). St Benedict here adapts Psalm 118:32 which, in the Vulgate, reads: "I have run the way of your commandments, because you have enlarged my heart". Once the capacity to love is extended, sluggishness is overcome and a new dynamism engendered. Like small children we have a surplus of energy: we won't walk when it's possible to run.

There is a summit to be attained in monastic experience. There is no question of an unending upward struggle with only a few plateaux that give a breathing-space. St Benedict describes this peak in terms of the simple concept of love. The heart is enlarged, love increases. When love becomes perfect then nothing can unseat it. Fear is banished and life loses its sense of being a burden. The winter has passed and a springtime of sober delight has begun.

St Benedict has introduced here a minor textual change that modifies the picture presented in Cassian and the Master. If we read the following texts closely we can see how the thought developed as it was passed from Cassian to the Master and as Benedict understood it.

*Inst 4.39.3*

When humility is possessed in truth, it will speedily lead you to the higher level which is the charity that has no fear. Through such [charity] you will begin to observe effortlessly, as if by nature, everything you used to perform with the pain of fear, no longer by contemplating punish-ment or by any fear, **but out of love of goodness itself and from delight in virtue.**

*RM 10.87-90*

After the disciple has climbed all these steps of humility he will have, in the fear of God, reached the top of the ladder, speedily arriving at that love of the Lord which, when perfect, casts out fear. Through such [charity] he will begin to observe effortlessly, as if by nature, everything he used to perform with fear, no longer from dread of hell, **but out of the love for the good habit itself and from delight in virtue.**

*RB 7.67-69*

Now, therefore, after ascending all these steps of humility, the monk will quickly arrive at that perfect love of God which casts out fear. Through this love, all that he used to observe somewhat fearfully, he will now begin to fulfill without effort, as though naturally from habit. **[He will act] no longer out of fear of hell, but out of love for Christ, from good habit itself and delight in virtue.**

Here we can see how close the three texts are, yet also how different. Benedict understands clearly that the monk is most intensely animated not by love of abstract goodness but by a personal love for Jesus Christ. "Let them prefer nothing to the love of Christ (RB 4.21; see 72.11). It is this love which, along with good habit and a progressive delight in virtue, becomes the source of all his actions. Good behavior no longer springs from fear and outward factors; it is an expression of inner reality. Human nature has been evangelized. The goal of monastic life, as was so amply appreciated by the medieval monks, is nothing less than the restoration in fallen human beings of the divine likeness. To the extent that this process is realized, the monk lives an evangelical life—a life in substantial accord with the teachings of Christ. Now is attained a genuine love that gives warmth to monastic observance. Now is it no longer a matter of doing violence to self in order to do the right thing. The good deeds that are the fruit of inner goodness flow easily and without having to be forced. The sign that a monk is growing strong in grace is the naturalness with which he performs those works that have their origin in grace. The conflict between spiritual aspiration and selfishness has been terminated. The monk has surrendered. His life is a testimony to the triumph of the Spirit.

~ 70 ~

*All this the Lord will by the Holy Spirit*
*graciously manifest in his workman*
*now cleansed of vice and sins.*

The credit for this spectacular change belongs to Christ. The monk is cognizant of having done nothing to merit it. It is Christ operating through the Holy Spirit that effects the miracle and permits it to become manifest. The process of divinization parallels that of purification. The ordinary workings of grace first separate the monk from his voluntary aberrations or sins and then continue by eradicating the sources of sin in his own unredeemed nature. There is a long period of pain in which the monk tames his will and allows himself to be purified. It demands action. For all the power of grace cannot counter human indifference. So the monk works hard to correspond with God's action. But he needs to keep in mind that it is God's work first. All that is accomplished in us is the effect of his saving compassion. Humility opens us to receive what God desires to give. What God gives us, above all, is mercy. No wonder St Benedict concludes his listing of the tools of the monk's trade: "Never to despair of God's mercy" (RB 4.74). The monk who has arrived at the top does not think in terms of his own achievement or success—he sees only the victory of God's grace.

## Concluding Remarks

We began this book by listing some of the objections made by late twentieth-century people to the whole concept of humility. While recognising the validity of many of these criticisms we have tried to show that the "humility" thus impugned is not what St Benedict and the monastic tradition have been advocating. Part of what I have hoped to achieve in compiling these reflections is the "rehabilitation" (if that is the right word) of St Benedict as one of the great spiritual masters and to demonstrate something of the vitality and viability of his spiritual approach.

Far from being demeaning or dehumanizing, true humility is a quality that enhances humanity. In St Benedict's view a monk is humble if meets the following criteria:

♦ he is serious in his commitment,
♦ he is free enough of inner conflict to be able to follow the way of Christ,
♦ he is able to endure the reverses and sufferings that are part of every human life,
♦ he is honest about himself,
♦ he is not ambitious or boastful,
♦ he does not hide behind a wall of talking and laughing,
♦ he is transparent in his goodness.

As St Paul would probably say, against such realities as these there can be no law.

I do not know if St Benedict would have enjoyed reading this book. While his text has been my starting point, I am aware that I have wandered some distance from his historical viewpoint. I have deliberately allowed myself to have been influenced both by subsequent monastic tradition (especially Bernard of Clairvaux) and by the needs and insights of our contemporaries. My hope is that these thoughts may help some to return to the text of Benedict's Rule and to find in it a springboard for their own reflection.

If I had to list some of the points I would hope might be remembered by the persevering reader, the following would come to mind.

a) Humility is not necessarily a bad thing, nor even indifferent, but an attitude that enhances both human life and spiritual endeavor.

b) As presented by St Benedict, humility is essentially the translation of Gospel values into the practical realities of daily monastic life.

c) Chapter 7 of the Rule is primarily descriptive and developmental. Benedict gives an account of the way a monk's spiritual life develops during the course of a lifetime.

d) This teaching is practical and experiential. It is not deduced from a theoretical base in anthropology or psychology. It speaks from experience with a view to shaping attitudes and influencing behaviour.

e) Although times have changed and human consciousness is different, there is much wisdom that can be distilled from these chapters.

f) I cannot speak with certainty, but it seems to me that Benedict's message on humility has application far beyond those who lead monastic lives. With appropriate qualifications I suspect that it would be helpful to any seekers after God.

g) Even if we are convinced that Benedict has an inadequate view of spiritual life as far as concerns modern women and men, I would suggest that he is worth listening to. Speaking of the deep realities of spiritual development from a different cultural perspective, he may have stumbled upon something that is hard to perceive from where we stand. We never know what falls within our blind spot, unless someone with a different blind spot can inform us.

h) Benedict's language and vocabulary may be unfamiliar and some of his themes, like the emphasis on sin, may be distasteful. I would aver that it is worth learning a new language to make contact with one of the spiritual giants of Christian history.

i) Benedict shows in Chapter 73 that he was under no illusion that he had covered all aspects of his subject or that he had said the last word on every topic concerning the life of monks. Let us take him literally. Let his Rule become for us a doorway to a tradition of life and thought that continues to have much to contribute to the present and future of the Church.

## Notes

[1] See M. Casey, "Intentio Cordis (RB 52.4)," *RBS* 6/7 (1977/78), pp. 105-120.

[2] See *The New Man* (London: Burns and Oates, 1962), pp. 15-16.

[3] Thomas Merton, "The Inner Experience: Notes on Contemplation (I)," *CSQ* 18.1 (1983), p. 7.

[4] Dil 27; SBOp 3,142.

[5] As they are also the dominant motifs to be found in the Book of Psalms.

[6] Bernard of Clairvaux, SC 18.6; SBOp 1.107.26.

*When man is truly humbled,*
*when he has learnt that he is not God,*
*then he is the nearest to becoming so.*
*In the end he may become so.*

--Patrick White, *Voss.*